Still I Rise

A Graphic History of African Americans

Roland Laird

with Taneshia Nash Laird

Illustrations by Elihu "Adolfo" Bey

Foreword by Charles Johnson

Historical consultants

Earl Lewis,
University of Michigan—Ann Arbor,
Department of History

Nell Painter, Princeton University,
Department of History

Produced by The Phillip Lief Group, Inc.

Still I Rise

A Graphic History of African Americans

STERLING

New York / London

www.sterlingpublishing.com

STERLING and the distinctive Sterling logo are registered trademarks of Sterling Publishing Co., Inc.

Library of Congress Cataloging-in-Publication Data

Laird, Roland Owen.
  Still I rise : a graphic history of African Americans / Roland Laird ; with Taneshia Nash Laird ; illustrations by Elihu "Adolfo" Bey ; foreword by Charles Johnson ; historical consultants: Earl Lewis, Nell Painter.
     p. cm.
  Subtitle of original edition: a cartoon history of African Americans.
  Includes bibliographical references.
  ISBN 978-1-4027-6226-0 (pbk. : alk. paper)
  1. African Americans--History--Caricatures and cartoons. I. Laird, Taneshia Nash. II. Bey, Elihu. III. Title.
  E185.L35 2009
  973'.0496073--dc22

2008031840

10 9 8 7 6 5 4 3 2 1

Published by Sterling Publishing Co., Inc.
387 Park Avenue South, New York, NY 10016

Revised edition published by Sterling Publishing Co., Inc. in 2009

Distributed in Canada by Sterling Publishing
c/o Canadian Manda Group, 165 Dufferin Street
Toronto, Ontario, Canada M6K 3H6

Sterling ISBN 978-1-4027-6226-0

For information about custom editions, special sales, premium and corporate purchases, please contact Sterling Special Sales Department at 800-805-5489 or specialsales@sterlingpublishing.com.

To our daughter Imani Fasarah Laird and to the
memory of her grandmother Ella Mae Dawson

Out of the huts of history's shame
I rise
Up from a past that's rooted in pain
I rise
I'm a black ocean, leaping and wide,
Welling and swelling I bear in the tide.

Leaving behind nights of terror and fear
I rise
Into a daybreak that's wondrously clear
I rise
Bringing the gifts that my ancestors gave,
I am the dream and the hope of the slave.
I rise
I rise
I rise.

From "Still I Rise"
Maya Angelou

Foreword:
A Capsule History of Blacks in Comics

Charles Johnson

*O*ne of the invaluable features of *Still I Rise*, the first cartoon history of black America, is the wealth of information its writers, Roland Laird and Taneshia Laird, and its artist Elihu Bey, provide about the marginalized—and often suppressed—political, economic and cultural contributions black people have made on this continent since the seventeenth century. Using the most basic means of communication we have—pictures—they transport us back through time, enabling us literally to see how dependent American colonists were on the agricultural sophistication of African slaves and indentured servants; how blacks fought and died for freedom during the Revolutionary and Civil Wars; and how, in ways both small and large, black genius shaped the evolution of democracy, the arts and sciences, and the English language in America, despite staggering racial and social obstacles.

As a contribution to illustrated history from a black point of view, *Still I Rise* is a unique achievement, one that will be valued—like Art Spiegelman's *Maus: A Survivor's Tale* and Larry Gonick's *A Cartoon History of the Universe*—by students, educators, collectors, and general readers for a long time to come. Yet it presents an interesting paradox. Although the book chronicles the often "invisible" history of black America in Elihu Bey's energetic and uncompromising drawings, the black men and women who were pioneers in the field of American comic art are noticeably absent. As a rule, cartoonists of any color often labor in obscurity. Except for a handful of current celebrities, among them Matt Groening ("The Simpsons"), Robert Crumb ("Fritz the Cat"), and Gary Larson ("The Far Side"), they are an unnamed, largely unrewarded tribe of ink-stained storytellers expressing themselves in a medium as ancient as that used by the Paleolithic painter who left images of reindeer grazing on the walls of a cave in Font-de-Gaume, France thirty thousand years ago. Remember: we think in pictures. Like music, the content of a drawing can be universally recognized; it cuts across language barriers, is "worth a thousand words," and has long been employed for tale-telling and propaganda. Regardless of age, nearly everyone recognizes the images of highly merchandized characters like Popeye and Superman, but how many of us can identify Elzie Segar, Joe Shuster and Jerry Siegal as their creators, or tell you much about them? This anonymity is, sad to say, even greater for the black comic artists who prepared the way for *Still I Rise*, although some of their creations have won an enduring place in America's popular imagination.

During a 1989 lecture trip in Germany for the United States Information Agency, I met one of those pioneers: the late, great Ollie Harrington, who died on November 2, 1995. Once called "America's favorite Negro cartoonist" by Langston Hughes, Harrington's weekly cartoon panel, "Dark Laughter," began its appearance in the *Amsterdam News* on May 25, 1935. By December 28, it was featuring Bootsie, a bald, pot bellied and witty observer of racial life (he could be the brother of Hughes's Jesse B. Semple) in one-panel drawings memorable not only for the crisp humor with which they laid bare social injustice but also for Harrington's delicate, detailed draftsmanship. (Vintage Harrington can be found in his cartoon depicting an elderly black scholar about to present his scientific research to white colleagues, one of whom benignly rests a hand on the scholar's shoulder, and says, "Doctor Jenkins, before you

read us your paper on inter-stellar gravitational tensions in thermo-nuclear propulsion, would you sing us a good old spiritual?")

Among Harrington's circle of friends during the Harlem Renaissance were writers Arna Bontemps, Rudolph Fisher and Wallace Thurman. He was the art director for Adam Clayton Powell's newspaper, the *People's Voice*, and, for the NAACP, he was a spokesman who assailed the lynchings of blacks in the south, a stance that brought him under the scrutiny of the F.B.I. In 1951, Harrington left America, joining a now legendary group of black expatriate artists that included Chester Himes and

"Doctor Jenkins, before you read us your paper on inter-stellar gravitational tensions in thermo-nuclear propulsion, would you sing us a good old spiritual?"

his close friend Richard Wright. But in 1961, a year after Wright's death, Harrington went to Berlin in August to speak with publishers about translating American classics and found himself trapped in East Berlin. In his essay, "Why I Left America," he wrote, "I couldn't leave because I didn't have the proper visas.... I was a virtual prisoner. I lost my French apartment. I lost everything. I had to stay there."[1] Yet still he worked for twenty years, placing his political drawings in the *Daily Worker* and East German magazines.

When the wall came down in the winter of 1989, East Berliners were flocking to the West. I learned Harrington was among them. Brimming with questions, I arranged to meet him at a cafe. An affable, friendly man, he arrived wearing a green turtleneck sweater, a brown leather jacket, and black-rimmed spectacles. Sipping coffee, we discussed Richard Wright's haiku and the situation of black cartoonists before he left the States. "Where," I asked, "did you publish your work?"

"That's the point," replied Harrington. "There wasn't anywhere to publish."

Of course, he was telling the truth. Before the 1960s, the great bulk of work by black cartoonists could be found only in black newspapers and magazines, and much of their effort has been lost or forgotten. To be sure, there were blacks in comics from nearly the beginning of the genre, which kicked off in America in 1896 with R. F. Outcault's "Yellow Kid." (Comic books came later, in May of 1934, the first being *Famous Funnies*.) But these black characters were grotesques—their faces, as Harrington once put it, "a circle, black with two hot dogs in the middle for a mouth."[2] There was Ebony, the buffoonish sidekick in Will Eisner's syndicated 1940s strip "The Spirit"; or the hulking Lothar, a black aide to "Phantom"-creator Lee Falk's "Mandrake the Magician." On and on from the late nineteenth century through the 1950s there were hideous, bubble-lipped Sambos penned by white illustrators influenced by Al Jolson and the minstrel tradition, and it was these vicious stereotypes that black comic artists, working primarily in the Negro press, fought mightily to correct.

Among these nearly forgotten creators is Jackie Ormes, one of the few black women cartoonists from the pre–Civil Rights era. Thanks to the research of comics historian Trina Robbins, author of *A Century of Women Cartoonists*, we know that Ormes's "Torchy Brown in Dixie and Harlem" premiered in 1937 on the pages of the *Pittsburgh Courier*, when she was twenty-two years old, and lasted until 1940, presenting over a three-year period the "Brenda Starr"–inspired adventures of her young heroine after she sells her farm and travels to New York City. For the *Chicago Daily Defender*, Ormes worked as a reporter in the 1940s and contributed an unpaid strip about a black maid called "Candy." Her single panel cartoon "Patty Jo 'n Ginger" was distributed by the Smith-Mann syndicate and in 1948 inspired Patty Jo dolls produced by the Terri Lee Co. in Nebraska; they were the first black character dolls in this country, Robbins reports, and are collector's items today. Ormes revived Torchy for the *Pittsburgh Courier* in a 1950 strip called "Torchy Brown Heartbeat," and in its panels tackled issues such as bigotry and pollution before the feature expired in 1955. Ormes died at age seventy in January 1987.[3]

To her credit, Robbins also unearthed the work of a second black woman cartoonist of the 1950s, Doris McClarty, whose one-page strip "Fireball Freddie" appeared in the black magazine *Hep*.[4] Its characters, slang-spouting hipsters, seemed drawn from the world of Cab Calloway. ("Well Pops," says one, "Kate gave me the gate. Now I'm doing the town brown.") However, students of the genre may find McClarty's work less interesting for its draftsmanship or ideas than for its linguistic curiosities—the discovery, for example, that black argot like "bust a cap" and "cop a plea" dates from the 1950s.

So yes, Harrington is correct about black cartoonists earlier in this century being confined largely to the black press. But was the reason simply the artists' race? Or was it that white editors and readers would not accept black content presented from a black point of view?[5] The evidence suggests the latter to be the case, at least in part, since black artists Russell Patterson and Matt Baker drew white characters in comics for mainstream publishers, and one of the most successful panel cartoonists of the 1940s and 1950s, E. Simms Campbell, published erotic humor so regularly in *Esquire* and *Playboy* that his elegant, painterly cartoons and clever gag lines significantly contributed to the urbane tone and visual style of those magazines. (In a quintessential Campbell drawing we find a smiling, sexually pleased white maid taking the fur wrap of her young, high society mistress, remarking, "While you were out, your Mr. Drake called—let's just call him our Mr. Drake from now on.") And to this list of black artists producing before the 1960s we must add the man whom art critic Gilbert Seldes identified in his 1924 book *The Seven Lively Arts* as being responsible for "the most amusing and fantastic and satisfying work of art produced in America today"[6]: George Herriman, the creator of "Krazy Kat."

For many readers and critics, among them E. E. Cummings, "Krazy Kat" was the greatest comic strip there ever was or would be. Pablo Picasso was a fan. Often described as the strip most preferred by intellectuals and savants, it ran in only about thirty-five newspapers (at its peak) from October 28, 1913, until Herriman's death on April 25, 1944. Yet for many fans "Krazy Kat" represented not merely the highest attainment of American comic art but a triumph of poetry, metaphysics, and democracy as well. Its premise was simple enough: Krazy, a black cat of indeterminate sex (but usually seen as female), loves Ignatz Mouse. But Ignatz hates Krazy and beans

the Kat on her noggin with a brick at every opportunity—an act the Kat always interprets as love ("a missil of affection"), thereby transcending the Mouse's hostility, even spiritualizing it in a way that would please both Mohandas K. Gandhi and Martin Luther King Jr. Completing this vaudevillian love triangle is Offissa Pupp, who loves Krazy, protects her from Ignatz, and frequently hauls the Mouse off to jail.

As with all great art, the simplicity of its premise conceals the many-layered complexities of "Krazy Kat." For poet Cummings this comic strip "reveals the ultimate meaning of existence."[7] In Ignatz he sees the spirit of free will tilting toward anarchy; in Offissa Pupp, the power of society and authority; and in Krazy he finds "a living ideal . . . the only original and authentic revolutionary protagonist. . . . She is a spiritual force," one who proved day after day in the papers of her most preeminent admirer, William Randolph Hearst, the truth of the adage "Love will find a way." And what has all this to do with democracy? Well, let us hear Cummings's own words: "The meteoric burlesk melodrama of democracy is a struggle between society (Offissa Pupp) and the individual (Ignatz Mouse) over an ideal (our heroine)—a struggle from which, again and again and again, emerges one stupendous fact: namely, that the ideal of democracy fulfills herself only if, and whenever, society fails to suppress the individual."[8]

Politics and metaphysics aside, Herriman's "Krazy Kat" was as revolutionary in its inventive compositions as in its ideas. Located in the dreamlike world of Coconino County, which recalls the artist's fondness for Monument Valley in the desert of southeastern Utah, Herriman's characters performed against a constantly transmogrifying background—in the space of two panels, their external world fluidly changed from surrealistic mesas and cactuses to forest scenery and seascapes, ever blurring the border between appearance and reality.

Herriman, a mulatto born in New Orleans in 1880, who according to reports never took off his hat,[9] indoors or out, because he had black, kinky hair, was a genuine American original. He experimented with the layouts for the Sunday panels of his strip, breaking down the conventional—and experiential—boundaries in the image area, a technique cartoonists would widely adopt thereafter. His scritchy penwork was joyously self-conscious, his characters aware that they lived in a comic strip—perhaps today we would call them "postmoderns," and his oeuvre "metacomic." He invested Krazy's voice with puns, poetry and linguistic playfulness, which usually earned her a brick on the head from Ignatz.

As so many have said, "Krazy Kat" cannot be explained; it simply must be experienced. And millions have absorbed this product of Herriman's genius; it was adapted as a ballet in 1922 by Adolph Bolm; inspired John Alden Carpenter's "jazz pantomime" for piano, numerous critical articles and anthologies, and Jay Cantor's 1988 *Krazy Kat: A novel in five panels*; and was included among the twenty ground-breaking "Comic Strip Classics" stamps issued by the U.S. Postal Service in 1995.

But if there is "black" content in "Krazy Kat," it is symbolic and covert. Not until the late 1960s, after the Civil Rights Movement and close on the heels of Stokely Carmichael's 1966 call for "Black Power" during a Mississippi march, do we witness an entire generation of black comic artists grappling with black content and themes.

According to grandmaster Harrington, one of the first to accept this challenge was Brumsic Brandon Jr. In his syndicated comic strip "Luther," Harrington says in a 1976 article, Brandon dared "to create non-white characters or even poor white characters who are human, sympathetic and even lovable. And what better stage setting could he devise than the schools and the kids they're trying to educate? Brandon buses his kids to the Alabaster Avenue Elementary School for their daily duels with Miss Backlash."[10]

In the 1960s and early 70s, however, the undisputed leader among syndicated black cartoonists was Morrie Turner, creator of "Wee Pals," a gentle, interracial comic strip about precocious children styled along the lines of (yet never as successful as) Charles Schulz's "Peanuts." By 1972 "Wee Pals" was appearing in seventy newspapers in the United States and abroad. But like the work of Harrington's generation, Turner's more biting social and racial cartoon commentary in the late 1960s and early 1970s was published—often in a panel called "Humor in Hue"—on the pages of

"Wrong salute, Private Jackson."

the black-owned press, in publications like the never financially profitable *Negro Digest* (later renamed *Black World* before its demise). A 1971 cartoon shows an elderly black man reading his newspaper at home. Then he notices a sinister-looking white man peering into his window and asks, "Are you the F.B.I., the C.I.A., Army intelligence or the welfare investigator?"

Turner was featured in the August 1972 issue of *Black World*. His work often kicked off that magazine's annual "cartoon festival," which frequently included work by younger cartoonists who signed their drawings with the names Pollard, Winners, Herb Roberts, Ham (who, if I'm not mistaken, also drew a panel for the Nation of Islam's *Muhammad Speaks*, creating white characters with devilish tails and horns), Dave Farmer, or Walt Carr a (highly versatile comic artist profiled in *Black World's* July 1973 issue), as well as cartoons of my own creation. Of all these contributors, Carr, a ten-year contributor to *Jet*, *Ebony*, and *Playboy* (which had the best rates for panel cartoonists at the time) was the most technically accomplished. Always his compositions were balanced, his lines bold and clean and economical like those of Hank Ketcham ("Dennis the Menace"), with a startlingly effective use of solid black shapes to pull a viewer's eye to his drawing's focal point. A typical Carr cartoon might show a seven-foot, militant, black high school student sitting on the sofa in his parents' home beside a white, baffled-looking college recruiter and saying, "Never mind the $100 a week job, new clothes and car, rent free apartment and job for father—will I get a degree?"

The early 70s was for black cartoonists, as it was for black people in general, a tumultuous, creative period. Some black gag-cartoonists like Buck Brown found steady work on the pages of *Playboy*.[11] New black magazines burst on the stands—providing new markets—and just as quickly disappeared. In that period, Tom Floyd, an Indiana-based editorial cartoonist who operated his own advertising firm, published *Integration Is a Bitch!* (1969), 116 pages of panel cartoons based on his experiences as a designer at Inland Steel Company. These were scathingly satirical drawings that explored the humiliations and pain endured by a black, white-collar worker decades before *Time* magazine devoted one of its covers to "The Rage of the Black Middle-Class." In one representative cartoon, a white employee shows his company's new black worker around the office as two white men from a mental institution drag off a Negro in a straitjacket. Says the white employee, "You'll be our second attempt at integration."

It was at this time that I worked full-time as a cartoonist, publishing around one thousand cartoons in the black press, in *Players*, the *Chicago Tribune* and other newspapers and selling one-page scripts to Charlton Comics. I also created two books, *Black Humor* (1970) and *Half-Past Nation Time* (1972), and created, hosted, and coproduced an early PBS how-to-draw series, "Charlie's Pad," which was broadcast nationally in 1970.

But what I shall call Harrington's Rule still applied—black content-cartoons in the 1970s were still difficult to place outside the black "special interest press," as some called it, and that rule is alive and well today. (Consider the *New Yorker's* special 1996 "Black in America" double issue, which featured the work of 13 "gag artists," only one of whom was black; eight blacks who submitted work were rejected, and the magazine's cartoon editor, Lee Lorenz, regretfully admits that the *New Yorker's* stable of cartoonists is still entirely white.)[12]

It would take another decade or two before we saw the efflorescence of an exciting new "Black Age of Comics," following or sprouting from the rise of so-called graphic novels (and Japanese manga) and stores devoted exclusively to comics, skyrocketing prices for comic art from the Golden and Silver Ages (on June 29, 1996, one of the fifty remaining copies of 1938's Action Comics #1, containing the first appearance of Superman, sold for $61,900 at Sotheby's), and the coming of age of a new generation of independent, Afrocentric, entrepreneurial cartoonist/publishers (there were about twenty nationwide in 1993) determined to market their own works directly to black readers. The names of these artists may be unknown to the larger public, but there can be no question that their products have propelled the long tradition of black cartooning into fresh, hitherto unexplored realms of the imagination.

A stroll through any well-stocked comics store in the 1990s might bring you into contact with the storytelling of Canadian artist Ho Che Anderson in *Black Dogs*, a meditation on the slaying of fifteen-year-old Latasha Harlins by a Korean storekeeper, the Rodney King beating, and Los Angeles riots; and his even more ambitious *King* (1993), a graphic novel about America's most preeminent Civil Rights leader. You may find Craig Rex Perry's *Hip Hop Heaven*, tales about black teenagers; or Brian and Wayne Cash's portrait of police brutality in *Harry the Cop*; or Turtel Onli's *Malcolm 10*, a comic about a clone possessing the brain of the slain Muslim leader (Onli also coined the term "Black Age of Comics"). If your luck prevails, there will be heroic adventure titles from ANIA, a consortium of black independent publishers who release Eric Griffith's *Ebony Warrior*; Rober Barnes's *Heru, Son of Ausar*; and *Zwanna, Son of Zulu*, by Nabile Hage, who, to promote his company, Dark Zulu, climbed the Georgia State Capitol building wearing a leopard-skin loincloth and tossed down comic books. Jason and David Sims's *Brotherman* may be on the shelves alongside issues of *Icon*, *Hardware*, and *Blood Syndicate*, superhero stories bearing the "Milestone" imprint, produced by black independents but distributed by D.C. comics.[13] If you can find them (or order them directly from their publishers), there is an embarrassment of black creative products to choose from—everything from Clint Walker's Christian "Faithwalker" comic strip to "Where I'm Coming From," a Jules Feiffer-esque syndicated feature by Barbara Brandon, daughter of the creator of "Luther"[14]; filmmaker Reginald Hudlin's *Bebe's Kids*, the first black feature-length animated film (based on characters by comedian

Robin Harris); and the ubiquitous Spike Lee's book *Floaters* produced with Dark Horse Comics.

Which brings us to Roland Laird's Posro Komics, founded in 1988 in Edison, N.J. The name "Posro" is a twist on "Negro," pointing to Laird's desire to bring a positive spirit to black comics production.[15] There are nine artists working in his stable to produce "MC Squared: A Man With a Serious Game Plan," a slice-of-life, hip-hop book featuring a young Harlem barber/computer hacker named Earl Terrel. In March 1993 Posro launched "The Griots," a witty strip about a black newspaper-owning family that was picked up by twenty newspapers. In one representative strip a black mother hears her daughter talking out loud, she thinks about the notorious Middle Passage: "Parents and children separated . . . human beings packed together and transported like cattle." The girl's mother is pleased, and thinks, "Wonderful . . . eleven years old and she already understands the horrors of slavery." Then she is mortified when her daughter continues: "A school bus can be a horrible experience."

Laird has stated, "We want to do the comic book equivalent of Invisible Man by Ralph Ellison, something that strong."[16] *Still I Rise* may very well be the realization of Posro's dream. Teamed with Elihu Bey, whose concern it is "to show the beauty in things that are not beautiful,"[17] Laird has contributed an epic to the field of American comic art, a transgenerational story that spans three centuries of racial and political oppression and the quest for freedom, a story inspirited by Olaudah Equiano's declaration that "When you make men slaves you compel them to live with you in a state of war."

Their task was formidable. Laird's script required exhaustive research, endless revisions, and was reviewed—one draft after another—by a team of historians and editors. But this challenge of compressing the broad, essential outlines of black American history into comic book format was only the first stage in creating *Still I Rise*. Regardless of how artful the script might be, the text for comic art must be seen as similar to a screenplay—it is essentially the starting point, or springboard, for stimulating the visual imagination of the illustrator, Elihu Bey, who, like a film director, must realize in images the writer's words one panel (or shot) at a time.

In film, before the cameras roll there is the storyboard, the director's carefully rendered "comic strip" that sketches out the possible sequence of shots in a movie. With a writer's script in hand, the illustrator's task closely resembles that of the director (and some filmmakers, such as Federico Fellini, came to film after first working as cartoonists). But for the comic artist there is no division of labor as in a film; he must be the director, cameraman, actors, set designer, make-up artist, hairdresser, and prop person all at once when he touches pencil to paper. Like a cameraman, he must decide which panels will provide "establishing shots," which will be close-ups or middle-istance, and where to locate the point of view—a bird's-eye angle looking down, or peering up from the floor, or reflecting the scene in a character's wine-glass or in a mirror, or from any unusual angle that will powerfully bring the writer's words to life. (As a playful exercise, compare the camerawork in *Citizen Kane* to the best draftsmanship of Will Eisner's "The Spirit" comics in the 1940s). Moreover, if he is inventive, there will be *movement* between his panels as he lays them out on the page, a kinetic feel or sense of flow that dynamically pulls the reader's eye from one panel to the next, a technique borrowed from the way many directors edit their shots. The movement of action (or "lines of force") in one shot may pull the viewer's eye from left to right, then in the following shot this direction may be immediately reversed, creating energy and tension (a device used often by James Cameron). Even before we read the text, we should feel excitement from the explosion of pictures on each page. We should find each panel so richly drawn, so charged with emotion in its smallest details, and so generous in the way the artist "fills the frame" that we constantly resist reading on too quickly in order to stop and study the panel for small revelations we might have missed at first glance.

Achieving this is every comic artist's dream, but such magic requires nothing less than throwing out reams of sketches before the illustrator settles on his final pencils for each page. He may do the inking himself, or rely on another artist's pen and brush work, for such collaborations often result in a startlingly elegant blend of visual styles (as when Wallace Wood brought his distinctive inking work to the pencils of Jack Kirby's comic strips in the 1950s). Then comes the lettering, which again the artist may farm out or do himself. Being an illustrator of many talents, young Elihu Bey chooses to draw, ink, and letter his own pages in this one-of-a-kind book.

Scenes of racial conflict are plentiful on the pages of *Still I Rise*, but as an illustration of American history from a black (and faintly Afrocentric) viewpoint we also find here a cornucopia of seldom-reported events, facts, and experiences of African-

Americans that enriches our understanding of this nation's past. More than a comic book or graphic novel (though it is indebted to both), *Still I Rise* is popular entertainment that enlightens. And permeating its encyclopedic research is Posro's recognition of the beauty, resilience, and spiritual endurance of black Americans who, refusing to lose faith in themselves and in the ideal of liberty, forced this republic time and again to live up to its principles of equality and justice.

Notes

1. Oliver W. Harrington, *Why I Left America and Other Essays* (Jackson: University Press of Mississippi, 1993).
2. Mel Watkins, "From Harlem to East Berlin," *N. Y. Times Book Review*, December 19, 1993.
3. All research on Jackie Ormes is from Trina Robbins, "Hidden Treasure," in *Comics Journal* (June 1993).
4. Trina Robbins, *A Century of Women Cartoonists* (Northampton, Mass.: Kitchen Sink Press, 1993).
5. Robbins, "Hidden Treasure."
6. Robert C. Harvey, *The Art of the Funnies: An Aesthetic History* (Jackson: University Press of Mississippi, 1994).
7. George Herriman, *Krazy Kat* (New York: Grosset & Dunlap, 1969).
8. Ibid.
9. Harvey, *The Art of the Funnies*.
10. Harrington, *Why I Left America*.
11. Richard Goldstein, "The Spin," *Village Voice*, May 7, 1996.
12. Ibid.
13. All research on black comic books is from Jeffrey Winbush's "The New Black Age of Comics," *Comics Journal* (June 1993).
14. Robbins, *A Century of Women Cartoonists*.
15. "At Posro Komics, Hip-Hop Heroes Battle Stereotypes," *New York Times*, July 12, 1993.
16. "Hip! Hop! Pow! The New Black Superheroes," *Washington Post*, October 13, 1991.
17. Gary Dauphin, "To Be Young, Superpowered, and Black," *Village Voice*, May 17, 1994.

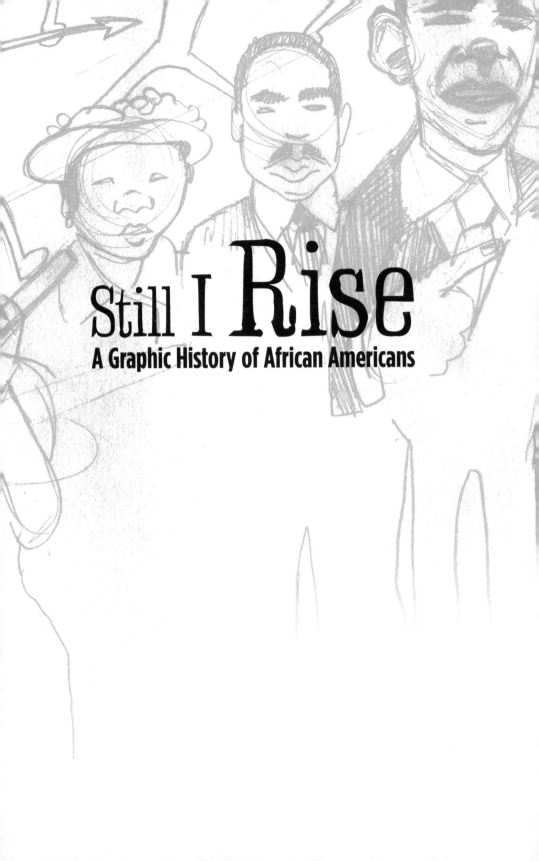

Still I Rise

A Graphic History of African Americans

AMERICA, THE RICHEST NATION ON THE FACE OF THE EARTH, HOME OF THE FREE, LAND OF THE BRAVE...

HOW DID IT GET THAT WAY? 'CAUSE AMERICA WAS THE LAND OF THE SLAVE. SLAVES CLEARED THE LAND, PLANTED THE FOOD, BUILT THE HOUSES, PAVED THE ROADS, AND...

...WAIT A SECOND, THAT'S NOT THE WHOLE STORY. YOU SEE, EARLY IN AMERICA'S COLONIAL DAYS, THE HARD LABOR WAS DONE BY PEOPLE WHO CONTRACTED THEMSELVES INTO BONDAGE FOR ANYWHERE FROM FOUR TO SEVEN YEARS, IN HOPES THAT AFTER THOSE YEARS THEY'D BE ABLE TO BUY THEIR OWN LAND. THEY WERE CALLED INDENTURED SERVANTS.

1618: JAMESTOWN, VIRGINIA

SOME WERE NATIVE AMERICANS, BUT MOST WERE EUROPEANS LOOKING FOR A WAY OUT OF POVERTY AND MISERY IN EUROPE. INSTEAD THEY FOUND MISERY AND POVERTY IN NORTH AMERICA.

COME NOW, WORK HARDER.

I'D'VE BEEN BETTER OFF KEEPIN' ME ARSE IN LONDON.

MEANWHILE THE COLONIAL MASTERS GREW GREEDY.

WITH MORE INDENTURED SERVANTS, I'LL BE ABLE TO BUY MORE WIGS.

AND THAT WAS THE BEGINNING OF A NORTH AMERICAN NIGHTMARE FOR AFRICAN PEOPLE.

1

WHEN THE AFRICANS ARRIVED IN JAMESTOWN, THEY WERE STRANGERS IN A STRANGE LAND.

THEY STRUGGLED WITH A STRANGE LANGUAGE,...

THIS IS CALLED A PLOW!

APLOW!

A STRANGE CLIMATE,...

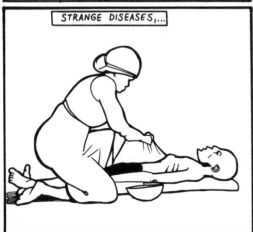

STRANGE DISEASES,...

AND STRANGE PEOPLE WITH STRANGE CLOTHES.

HERE, TRY THIS HAT ON.

BUT THE COLONIAL MASTERS HAD GOTTEN MORE THAN THEY EXPECTED. AFRICANS WERE NOT ONLY EXPERT FARMERS BUT SHREWD BUSINESS PEOPLE. SOME QUICKLY WORKED THEIR WAY OUT OF INDENTURED SERVITUDE.

FREEDOM FROM INDENTURE DID NOT FREE THE FORMER SERVANTS FROM HUMAN WEAKNESSES. A NUMBER OF THEM FORMED THEIR OWN PLANTATIONS WITH THEIR OWN INDENTURED SERVANTS.

THEY DIDN'T EVEN SAY GOODBYE.

PURNT!

ANTHONY AND MARY JOHNSON WERE AN AFRICAN COUPLE WHO BOUGHT OUT THEIR INDENTURE IN 1624. BY THE EARLY 1650s, THEY OWNED A 250-ACRE SPREAD IN NORTHAMPTON COUNTY, VIRGINIA, WITH BLACK AND WHITE SERVANTS.

THAT DIDN'T SIT TOO WELL WITH A LOT OF WHITE PEOPLE.

WHEN YOU'RE FINISHED PLOWING, SMITTY I'M GOING TO NEED YOU TO CHOP SOME WOOD.

I'D LIKE IT FINISHED WHEN I GET BACK.

A WHITE MAN LIKE YOU DON'T NEED TO BE TAKIN' ORDERS FROM A BLOODY NIGGER.

HE'S ME BOSS, GUV'NAH

I GOT NO CHOICE.

BESIDES, HE'S A GOOD MAN.

THAT BLACK BASTARD'S NO MORE A MAN THAN MY MULE. I CAN SEE YOU'VE GOT A LOT TO LEARN, FRIEND.

6

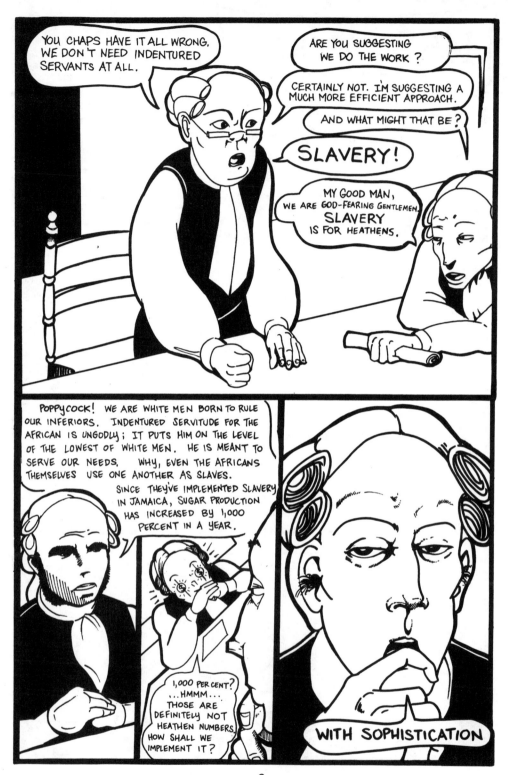

8

SOPHISTICATED MEANT SNEAKY, LOW-DOWN AND DIRTY.

1646: VIRGINIA

IN JUST THREE WEEKS WE'LL BE FREE.

YES INDEED, GUY'NAH. HAVE YA GOT ANY PLANS?

YEH, I HEAR AFRICANS HAVE ESTABLISHED A HOMELAND IN A PLACE CALLED FLORIDA.

THAT'S WHERE I'M GOIN'.

THREE WEEKS LATER

AT LAST, FREEDOM.

YES, AT LAST.

THANK YOU FOR YOUR YEARS OF EFFORT. YOU'RE FREE TO LEAVE.

YOU, ON THE OTHER HAND, MUST STAY.

WHAT?!

9

10

BUT RUNNING AWAY WITH WHITES DIDN'T WORK OUT EITHER. WHEN WE GOT CAUGHT, OUR CONTRACTS WERE EXTENDED INDEFINITELY. IT WAS ALL PART OF THE PLAN TO MAKE BLACK FOLKS **SLAVES FOR LIFE.** THE WHITE FOLKS THAT GOT CAUGHT HAD THEIR CONTRACTS EXTENDED TOO, BUT NOT FOR AS LONG.

THAT'S THE LAST TIME I DO ANYTHING WITH A NIGGER.

BLACK PEOPLE LOOKED FOR WAYS TO FIGHT EXTENDED CONTRACTS AND THE SPECTER OF A LIFETIME OF SLAVERY.

THESE BUCKRAS AIN'T DEALIN' FAIR. THEY JUST EXTEND OUR WORK TIME WHENEVER THEY FEEL LIKE IT.

TRUE. AND DON'T EVEN TRY RUNNIN' AWAY 'CAUSE IF THEY CATCH YA THEN THEY MAKE YOU WORK FOR 'EM FOR THE REST OF YOUR DAYS.

WE STILL GOT ANOTHA' CHANCE TO BE FREE.

OH YEAH, LIKE WHAT?

THE COURTS.

THESE BUCKRAS GOT RULES THAT THEY BREAKIN'. WE COULD SUE FOR OUR FREEDOM.

BROTHER, WHERE YOU BEEN? SOME OF US FURTHER DOWN THE ROAD TRIED THAT. IT DIDN'T WORK. SOMEBODY EVEN SUED A FREE AFRICAN BY THE NAME OF ANTHONY JOHNSON, TO GET OUTTA A CONTRACT HE KEPT EXTENDING. STILL DIDN'T WORK.

13

14

15

MANY OF THE SLAVES SAW. THE REBELLION AS A STEP TOWARD FREEDOM.

WHAT THEY DIDN'T SEE WAS THE REBELLION'S ORIGIN. A WHITE TRADER ACCUSED OF CHEATING NATIVE AMERICANS WAS ATTACKED; THE WHITES' RETALIATION WAS USED BY BACON AS AN EXCUSE TO KILL NATIVE AMERICANS AND TAKE THEIR LAND. GOVERNOR BERKELEY SAW BACON'S AGGRESSION AS INSUBORDINATION, SO BACON AND HIS REBELS TURNED ON BERKELEY AND THE COLONIAL OVERLORDS, AND TRIED TO SEIZE THEIR LAND AS WELL.

ONCE THE WHITES STARTED FIGHTING EACH OTHER AND NOT JUST THE NATIVE AMERICANS, BACON'S REBELLION WAS PUT DOWN BY THE VIRGINIAN ELITE AND THE BLACKS GOT PUT BACK INTO SLAVERY.

GENTLEMEN, EVERY CLOUD HAS A SILVER LINING, AND NATHANIEL BACON'S REBELLION WAS NO EXCEPTION.

BETTER BE A DAMN FINE SILVER. WE NEARLY LOST ALL OUR PROPERTY.

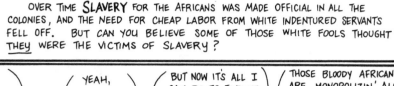

OVER TIME **SLAVERY** FOR THE AFRICANS WAS MADE OFFICIAL IN ALL THE COLONIES, AND THE NEED FOR CHEAP LABOR FROM WHITE INDENTURED SERVANTS FELL OFF. BUT CAN YOU BELIEVE SOME OF THOSE WHITE FOOLS THOUGHT <u>THEY</u> WERE THE VICTIMS OF SLAVERY?

YOU KNOW, WHEN THEY STARTED THIS WHOLE AFRICAN SLAVERY THING, I THOUGHT LIFE'D BE A BREEZE.

YEAH, I THOUGHT ME DAYS OF SCRAMBLIN' WAS OVER.

BUT NOW IT'S ALL I CAN DO TO FIND ME AN HONEST DAY'S WORK.

THOSE BLOODY AFRICANS ARE MONOPOLIZIN' ALL THE WORK, AND I CAN'T EVEN FILL ME BELLY.

THERE'S NO WAY I'M GWINE LET YOU WORK YOSELF TA DEATH. YOU JUS' REST SOME. I'LL KEEP ON.

JUST LOOK AT THAT SLACKIN' NIGGER OVER THERE.

IF I WAS THEIR MASTER, I'D MAKE SURE THEY WORK.

EXCUSE ME, BUT I COULDN'T HELP BUT HEAR YOUR CONVERSATION. I HAVE A PROPOSITION FOR YOU.

BRUTALITY LIKE THAT SOMETIMES PROVOKED RETALIATION.

AND WHEN THE SLAVES RETALIATED, THEY WERE PUNISHED.

22

23

BUT ON FARMS AND PLANTATIONS IN THE NORTH AND SOUTH SOME MASTERS USED OVERSEERS TO WORK THEIR PROPERTY HALF TO DEATH.

24

NOW THAT THE SCREWS OF SLAVERY WERE TIGHT, MORE SHIPS SAILED TO THE SHORES OF AFRICA QUESTING FOR 'BLACK GOLD' ON A REGULAR BASIS, AND THE BRUTALITY THAT FOLLOWED MADE THE AFRICANS' PRIOR EXPERIENCES IN INDENTURED SERVITUDE LOOK LIKE PARADISE.

THEY WERE SHACKLED AND PACKED TOGETHER ON THE SLAVE SHIPS LIKE RATS.
FOR THE FIRST FEW DAYS ABOARD, THE SLAVES REMAINED SHACKLED TO ONE ANOTHER, CHAINED AND BOLTED TO THE SHIP. UNABLE TO MOVE ABOUT, THEY WERE FORCED TO RELIEVE THEMSELVES ON THEMSELVES.

IT WAS IN THESE MOST ODIOUS CONDITIONS THAT THE SEEDS OF AFRICAN RESISTANCE WERE SOWN.

AS THE JOURNEY OF THE SHIP CONTINUED, THE AFRICANS WERE OCCASIONALLY BROUGHT FOR A FEW MINUTES TO THE TOP DECK OF THE SHIP FOR SUNLIGHT AND EXERCISE. THIS WAS NOT A MORAL CONSIDERATION BUT MERELY A BUSINESS DECISION, BECAUSE AFTER ALL, THE SHIP'S CREWS WERE BEING PAID TO BRING BACK HEALTHY SLAVES. STILL, HUNDREDS OF THOUSANDS OF CAPTIVE AFRICANS DIED IN TRANSIT.

28

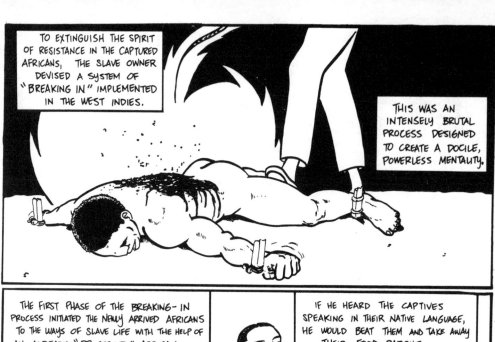

TO EXTINGUISH THE SPIRIT OF RESISTANCE IN THE CAPTURED AFRICANS, THE SLAVE OWNER DEVISED A SYSTEM OF "BREAKING IN" IMPLEMENTED IN THE WEST INDIES.

THIS WAS AN INTENSELY BRUTAL PROCESS DESIGNED TO CREATE A DOCILE, POWERLESS MENTALITY.

THE FIRST PHASE OF THE BREAKING-IN PROCESS INITIATED THE NEWLY ARRIVED AFRICANS TO THE WAYS OF SLAVE LIFE WITH THE HELP OF AN ALREADY "PROCESSED" AFRICAN, KNOWN AS A SLAVE DRIVER.

THE SLAVE DRIVER GAVE THE NEW ARRIVALS CLOTHES AND TAUGHT THEM SIMPLE ENGLISH.

IF HE HEARD THE CAPTIVES SPEAKING IN THEIR NATIVE LANGUAGE, HE WOULD BEAT THEM AND TAKE AWAY THEIR FOOD RATIONS.

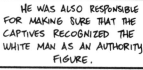

ASANTE SANA

I TOLD YOU, DON'T SPEAK THAT AFRICAN STUFF HERE!

HE WAS ALSO RESPONSIBLE FOR MAKING SURE THAT THE CAPTIVES RECOGNIZED THE WHITE MAN AS AN AUTHORITY FIGURE.

WHEN A WHITE MAN TALKS TO YOU, YOU BEST NOT MOVE A MUSCLE.

30

IN MY LAND, THIS SOIL WOULD BE PERFECT FOR GROWING RICE.

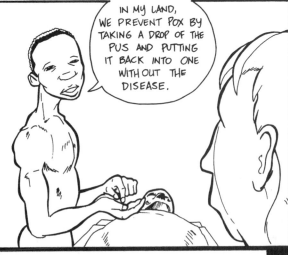

IN MY LAND, WE PREVENT POX BY TAKING A DROP OF THE PUS AND PUTTING IT BACK INTO ONE WITHOUT THE DISEASE.

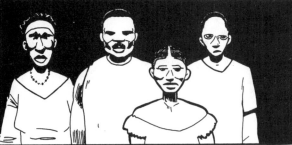

EVEN UNDER THE WORST CIRCUMSTANCES, AFRICANS STILL FOUND WAYS TO SHOW THEIR INGENUITY. THEY BROUGHT ADVANCED METHODS OF RICE GROWING AND AN INOCULATION FOR SMALL POX TO THESE SHORES. FOR THESE CONTRIBUTIONS THERE WAS NO GUARANTEE OF REWARD.

BUT IF THEY BETRAYED EACH OTHER, REWARD WAS ALMOST ASSURED.

YA DONE GOOD, BOY.

STILL, MOST SLAVES TRIED TO LOOK OUT FOR ONE ANOTHER AND WORK TOGETHER.

THEY STARTED FAMILIES.

WHENEVER POSSIBLE THEY SOCIALIZED.

MOST IMPORTANTLY THEY NEVER, EVER LOST HOPE.

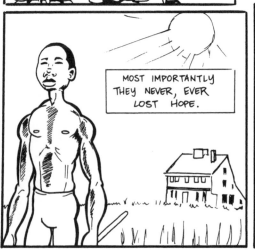

EACH YEAR MORE AND MORE AFRICANS ARRIVED ON THE SHORES OF NORTH AMERICA, AND MANY OF THEM FOUGHT ENSLAVEMENT VIGOROUSLY.

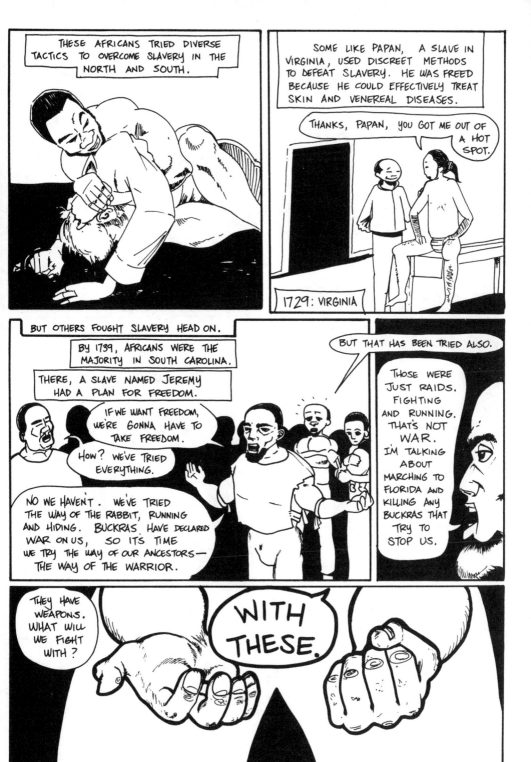

THESE AFRICANS TRIED DIVERSE TACTICS TO OVERCOME SLAVERY IN THE NORTH AND SOUTH.

SOME LIKE PAPAN, A SLAVE IN VIRGINIA, USED DISCREET METHODS TO DEFEAT SLAVERY. HE WAS FREED BECAUSE HE COULD EFFECTIVELY TREAT SKIN AND VENEREAL DISEASES.

THANKS, PAPAN, YOU GOT ME OUT OF A HOT SPOT.

1729: VIRGINIA

BUT OTHERS FOUGHT SLAVERY HEAD ON.

BY 1739, AFRICANS WERE THE MAJORITY IN SOUTH CAROLINA.

THERE, A SLAVE NAMED JEREMY HAD A PLAN FOR FREEDOM.

IF WE WANT FREEDOM, WE'RE GONNA HAVE TO TAKE FREEDOM.

HOW? WE'VE TRIED EVERYTHING.

NO WE HAVEN'T. WE'VE TRIED THE WAY OF THE RABBIT, RUNNING AND HIDING. BUCKRAS HAVE DECLARED WAR ON US, SO ITS TIME WE TRY THE WAY OF OUR ANCESTORS— THE WAY OF THE WARRIOR.

BUT THAT HAS BEEN TRIED ALSO.

THOSE WERE JUST RAIDS. FIGHTING AND RUNNING. THAT'S NOT WAR. I'M TALKING ABOUT MARCHING TO FLORIDA AND KILLING ANY BUCKRAS THAT TRY TO STOP US.

THEY HAVE WEAPONS. WHAT WILL WE FIGHT WITH?

WITH THESE.

35

WHAT IN GOD'S NAME DO YOU NIGRAS THINK YOU'RE DOIN'? IF YOU KNOW WHAT'S GOOD FOR YOU, Y'ALL WILL GET BACK TO YOUR MASTERS.

ANSWER ME, NIGRA!

ON TO FLORIDA, MEN!

THE INSURRECTION LASTED ONE DAY, AND IN THE END THE STONO UPRISING WAS PUT DOWN VIOLENTLY.

JEREMY AND HIS CREW HAD GOOD REASON TO RISK DEATH TO GET TO FLORIDA. ESCAPED SLAVES KNOWN AS "MAROONS" AND NATIVE AMERICAN REFUGEES FROM THE CREEK NATION CALLING THEMSELVES "SEMINOLES" WERE AMONG FLORIDA'S FIRST SETTLERS.

TOGETHER THEY BUILT UP THE SEMINOLE NATION...

...DESPITE DENSE JUNGLES AND WILDLIFE...

...AND HOSTILE ENCOUNTERS WITH SPANISH SETTLERS.

BUT THE RED AND BLACK SEMINOLES PERSEVERED, AND BY 1741 THE COMMUNITY KNOWN AS GARCIA REAL DE SANTA TERESA IN ST. AUGUSTINE, FLORIDA, HAD BECOME A LARGE SEMINOLE SETTLEMENT.

BUT THAT WAS SOON GOING TO CHANGE...

38

DESPITE SLAVERY'S OMINOUS PRESENCE THROUGHOUT THE COLONIES, MANY FREE AFRICANS ACHIEVED GREAT THINGS.

EMMANUEL BERNOON WAS A SUCCESSFUL CATERER AND OYSTER HOUSE OWNER IN RHODE ISLAND.

LUCY TERRY OF MASSACHUSETTS WAS ONE OF THE MOST POPULAR STORYTELLERS IN NEW ENGLAND.

IN MARYLAND, BENJAMIN BANNEKER BUILT THE FIRST STRIKING CLOCK WHOLLY OF AMERICAN-MADE PARTS. IT KEPT PERFECT TIME FOR 40 YEARS

AND FOR EVERY BERNOON, TERRY, AND BANNEKER, THERE WERE THOUSANDS OF AFRICANS IN THE NORTH AND SOUTH STRUGGLING TO GIVE MEANING, PURPOSE AND BEAUTY TO THE LIFE OF BRUTALITY THAT THEY WERE CONSIGNED TO.

41

THAT VERDICT DID NOT DISCOURAGE SLAVES AND, AS THE YEARS PASSED, THEY CONTINUED TO FIGHT FOR THEIR FREEDOM. SOON THEIR DESIRE FOR FREEDOM AND THE WHITE COLONISTS' DESIRE FOR THEIR OWN INDEPENDENT NATION MET IN THE PERSON OF A RUNAWAY BLACK SLAVE NAMED CRISPUS ATTUCKS.

1770: BOSTON

PROTEST BRITISH OPPRESSION

THESE LIMEY REDCOATS ARE EVERYWHERE.

SOMEBODY OUGHT TO DO SOMETHIN' ABOUT THEM.

IF YOU BLOKES WANT TO END TYRANNY, YOU HAVE TO BE WILLING TO CONFRONT TYRANNY. THAT'S HOW I GOT MY FREEDOM.

JEEZ, CRISPUS, I AIN'T IN THE MOOD FOR ANOTHER ONE OF YOUR RUNAWAY SLAVE STORIES.

JOKE IF YOU WANT, BUT I'M TAKING A STAND.

WAIT, CRISPUS! HAVE YA GONE MAD?

IF WE WANT TO GET RID OF THE REDCOATS, WE MUST ATTACK THE MAIN GUARD!

MARCH 5, 1770: BOSTON

NOBODY CAN SAY FOR SURE WHAT MOTIVATED CRISPUS ATTUCKS TO RUSH THE REDCOATS, BUT HE WAS THE FIRST MAN TO DIE IN THE STRUGGLE FOR COLONIAL FREEDOM.

HIS DEATH HELPED CRACK OPEN A SHORT-LIVED WINDOW OF OPPORTUNITY FOR BLACK PEOPLE IN THE STRUGGLE FOR FREEDOM.

IN 1773, A MASSACHUSETTS SLAVE NAMED CAESAR HENDRICKS WON A COURT CASE AGAINST HIS ENSLAVER FOR DETAINING HIM IN SLAVERY. NOT ONLY WAS HE GRANTED HIS FREEDOM, BUT HE GOT DAMAGES TO BOOT.

YES!

BUT FREEDOM MEANT DIFFERENT THINGS TO DIFFERENT PEOPLE, AND AT THE SAME TIME THAT SOME SLAVES SOUGHT FREEDOM THROUGH THE COURTS, OTHERS LOOKED TO A HIGHER AUTHORITY.

WE AFRICANS WERE A DEEPLY SPIRITUAL PEOPLE LONG BEFORE WE SET FOOT IN NORTH AMERICA.

BUT 150 YEARS OF AMORALITY PUT OUR SPIRIT TO THE TEST.

STILL, WE FOUND INNOVATIVE WAYS TO EXPRESS OUR SENSE OF DIVINITY.

WE SANG IN THE FIELDS TO MAKE OUR LOADS LIGHTER.

OUR WORK SONGS BECAME SPIRITUALS.

SOMETIMES WE GATHERED INFORMALLY TO WORSHIP IN TRADITIONAL RELIGIONS LIKE YORUBA AND AKAN, BUT WHEN LAWS WERE PASSED LIMITING THE ASSEMBLY OF BLACKS AND THE USE OF DRUMS, OUR GATHERINGS WERE EFFECTIVELY BANNED.

THOUGH WHITES STOPPED US FROM WORSHIPPING IN OUR OWN GROUPS, MANY OF OUR ENSLAVERS DIDN'T OBJECT TO US WORSHIPPING WITH THEM IN A "CHRISTIAN" MANNER.

YOU SEE, WHITE FOLKS USED CHRISTIANITY TO KEEP BLACK FOLKS DOWN.

BUT MANY CHRISTIAN SLAVES BELIEVED THAT JUDGMENT DAY WAS COMING TO THEIR ENSLAVERS, AND ON THAT DAY, A CHANGE WAS GONNA COME.

THE LETTER OF PAUL TO THE EPHESIANS CLEARLY STATES THAT WE SHOULD TEACH SLAVES TO OBEY THEIR MASTERS.

THE REJECTED ONE SHALL BE THE CORNERSTONE OF THE NEW FOUNDATION.

THE DIFFERENCES IN HOW AND WHY BLACK PEOPLE WORSHIPPED DROVE SOME OF US TO BUILD OUR OWN CHURCHES. IN SILVER BLUFF, SOUTH CAROLINA, THE FIRST BAPTIST CHURCH UNDER AFRICAN AMERICAN LEADERSHIP WAS BUILT IN 1773.

GOD BLESS THE CHILD THAT'S GOT HIS OWN.

THERE WAS WHITE RESISTANCE TO THE CONSTRUCTION OF THE CHURCH IN SILVER BLUFF AND OTHERS LIKE IT. BUT IN THE END, THE ENSLAVERS HAD MORE AMBITIOUS THINGS ON THEIR MINDS.

WE'VE GOT A NATION TO BUILD. WE HAVEN'T GOT TIME TO WORRY ABOUT NEGROES GOING TO CHURCH.

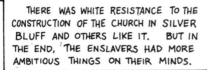

BY 1776, WHITE COLONISTS HAD FOUGHT MANY BATTLES WITH THE BRITISH. ON THE FRONT LINES, MEN LIKE PETER SALEM, SALEM POOR, AND PRINCE HALL FOUGHT AND KILLED MANY BRITISH FOR THE CAUSE OF "AMERICAN FREEDOM."

MAYBE NOW THEY'LL SEE ME AS AN EQUAL.

IN PHILADELPHIA IN 1776, WHITE COLONISTS MET TO DECLARE THEIR INDEPENDENCE FROM BRITAIN. THEY ALSO DISCUSSED AFRICANS' STATUS AS SLAVES.

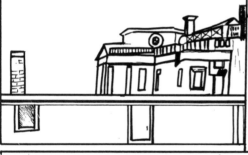

WE CANNOT LEGITIMATELY DECLARE OURSELVES A RIGHTEOUS AND JUST NATION WHILE ENSLAVING OUR AFRICAN BRETHREN.

IF WE FREE ALL THE AFRICANS, WHAT DO YOU PROPOSE WE DO WITH THEM, MR. JEFFERSON? ALREADY THE FREE ONES COMPETE WITH WHITE MEN FOR JOBS.

YES, MR. JEFFERSON, MR. MADISON IS RIGHT. BESIDES, IF WE LOOK AROUND THE NORTH, HASN'T SLAVERY ALL BUT DIED OUT? WHY DON'T WE JUST LET NATURE TAKE IT'S COURSE AND LET SLAVERY DIE A NATURAL DEATH?

PERHAPS...

THANK YOU. NOW LET US GET ON WITH THE BUSINESS AT HAND.

47

BACK IN PHILADELPHIA...

GENTLEMEN, AFRICANS ALL OVER THE COLONIES ARE RUNNING AWAY TO JOIN THE BRITISH. WE HAVE NO CHOICE BUT TO MATCH THE BRITISH OFFER.

GEORGE WASHINGTON

SKRATCH! SKRATCH!

BRITISH ARMY

AMERICAN ARMY

BY 1778, SOME BLACKS WERE JOINING THE AMERICAN ARMY, TOO, AS THEY HAD BEFORE 1776.

STILL, MANY BLACK PEOPLE KNEW THAT ENLISTING IN ARMIES WAS NOT A TRUE KEY TO FREEDOM.

FIGHTIN' FOR THESE WHITE FOLKS MIGHT GET SOME OF OUR MEN FREE. BUT WHAT ABOUT US WOMEN?

YES, AND WHAT ABOUT THE CHILDREN AND THE OLD FOLKS?

RECOGNIZING THE LIMITATIONS OF ENLISTMENT, ONE WOMAN BENT THE RULES.

IF IT'S A MAN THEY WANT, IT'S A MAN THEY'LL GET.

FOR 17 LONG MONTHS, DEBORAH GANNET POSED AS A MAN IN THE CONTINENTAL ARMY. EVEN IN FIGHTING FOR FREEDOM, SHE WASN'T FREE TO BE HERSELF.

EVENTUALLY THE COLONIES DID WIN THEIR FREEDOM, AND A NEW NATION WAS BORN. DURING THE WAR, SLAVERY WAS ABOLISHED IN TWO STATES— VERMONT AND MASSACHUSETTS— AND MANY SLAVES GAINED THEIR FREEDOM. TWENTY THOUSAND SLAVES LEFT THE COLONIES WITH THE BRITISH AND WERE FREED IN THE WEST INDIES. THOUSANDS MORE ESCAPED TO THE RANKS OF FREE AFRICANS IN THE NEW NATION KNOWN AS THE **UNITED STATES OF AMERICA.** BUT THE VAST MAJORITY REMAINED ENSLAVED.

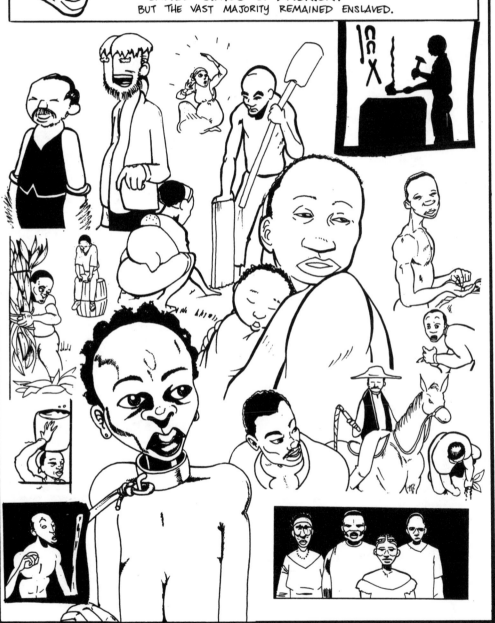

EVEN FREEDOM HAD ITS CHALLENGES.

IN PHILADELPHIA, MEN LIKE ABSALOM JONES AND RICHARD ALLEN, BOTH FORMER SLAVES, REALIZED THE NEED FOR AFRICAN SOLIDARITY. THEY STARTED THE FREE AFRICAN SOCIETY, A MUTUAL-AID ORGANIZATION THAT RAISED MONEY FOR ORPHANS AND HELPED THE SICK AND THE NEEDY.

1787: PHILADELPHIA

1787: BOSTON

IN NEW ENGLAND, SUCH SOLIDARITY COULD NOT PREVENT MANY FREE BLACKS FROM BEING CAPTURED AND RE-ENSLAVED.

YOU'RE COMIN' WITH US, NIGGER.

1788: BOSTON

SINCE THE END OF THE WAR WE'VE KEPT TO OURSELVES. WE'VE BEEN GOOD CITIZENS. WE'VE STARTED OUR OWN MUTUAL-AID ORGANIZATIONS LIKE THE MASONS. YET STILL WE HAVE HAD TO FIGHT FOR EVERYTHING. FIRST IT WAS EQUAL SCHOOLS FOR OUR CHILDREN. NOW AGAIN WE SEE SOME OF OUR OWN PEOPLE TAKEN AND ENSLAVED RIGHT BEFORE OUR EYES. I DID NOT FIGHT IN THE WAR SO THAT MY PEOPLE COULD LIVE LIKE BOAT RATS! WE WILL TAKE THIS TO THE COURTS, AND IF THAT DOES NOT WORK WE WILL TAKE IT TO THE STREETS.

PRINCE HALL

SOME OF THE FREE BLACK POPULATION WANTED NO PART OF SO-CALLED **AMERICAN FREEDOM.**

WHAT GOOD IS IT BEING FREE IN AMERICA IF WE MUST LOOK OVER OUR SHOULDERS AT EVERY TURN? MOST OF US ARE STILL SLAVES. WHO IS TO SAY THAT ONE DAY WE WILL NOT BE SLAVES AGAIN? WE SHOULD RETURN TO AFRICA.

INDEED WE SHOULD.

A YEAR EARLIER, PRINCE HALL HAD LED THE EFFORT TO PETITION THE MASSACHUSETTS GOVERNMENT FOR EQUAL SCHOOL FACILITIES FOR BLACK FOLK. NOW HE LED THE BLACK COMMUNITY IN BOSTON IN FORCING THE MASSACHUSETTS GOVERNMENT TO FREE BLACKS WHO HAD BEEN RE-ENSLAVED.

WHILE SOME BLACK FOLK DEBATED, WHITE FOLK BEGAN THE TASK OF FORGING A GOVERNMENT AT THE CONSTITUTIONAL CONVENTION OF 1787.

... SIMPLY PUT, WE SOUTHERNERS BELIEVE THE NUMBER OF OUR REPRESENTATIVES IN THE CONGRESS SHOULD BE BASED ON OUR STATES' **TOTAL** POPULATION, INCLUDING SLAVES; BUT THAT OWNERSHIP OF SLAVES SHOULD NOT BE TAXED.

WE IN THE NORTH HOLD THE CONTRARY VIEW: SLAVES SHOULD BE COUNTED FOR PURPOSES OF TAXATION, BUT NOT FOR DETERMINING ANY STATE'S REPRESENTATION IN CONGRESS.

TO SETTLE THIS MATTER, I PROPOSE THAT FOR PURPOSES OF BOTH TAXATION AND REPRESENTATION, EACH SLAVE BE COUNTED AS THREE-FIFTHS OF A MAN.

SOON AFTER, THE THREE-FIFTHS COMPROMISE BECAME THE LAW OF THE LAND.

THREE-FIFTHS OF A MAN, BUT FIVE-THIRDS OF THE WORK.

THE FEDERAL NORTHWEST ORDINANCE OF 1787 STATED THAT SLAVERY WOULD NOT BE ALLOWED TO SPREAD TO THE TERRITORY BOUNDED BY THE MISSISSIPPI AND THE OHIO RIVERS. BUT THE ORDINANCE HIGHLIGHTED A PRICKLY ISSUE—IN A GIVEN TERRITORY OR STATE, WHO WOULD HAVE MORE POWER, THE LOCAL GOVERNMENT, OR THE FEDERAL GOVERNMENT? AS THAT ARGUMENT EBBED AND FLOWED, THE SOUTHERN ELITE HELD ON TO SLAVERY FOR DEAR LIFE.

THEN, IN 1793, AN INVENTION BREATHED NEW LIFE INTO SOUTHERN SLAVERY:

ELI WHITNEY'S COTTON GIN.

THE DEMAND FOR SLAVES IN THE SOUTH WENT THROUGH THE ROOF AND OUR HARD TIMES GOT HARDER AND LONGER.

BUT THE DESIRE OF THE CHILDREN OF AFRICA TO BE FREE WAS JUST AS STRONG AS THE DESIRE OF THE SLAVEHOLDERS TO KEEP THEM ENSLAVED. SOME SLAVES, LIKE JOHN C. STANLEY OF CRAVEN COUNTY, NORTH CAROLINA, WERE ABLE TO BUY THEIR FREEDOM.

WORKING AS A BARBER, STANLEY HAD AMASSED A CONSIDERABLE AMOUNT OF WEALTH.

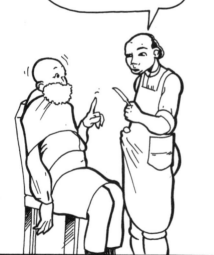

... HE INVESTED IN SOME PLANTATIONS — BUT WITH CONDITIONS.

ONLY IF YOU FREE HALF OF YOUR SLAVES WILL I INVEST IN YOUR COTTON PLANTATION.

BUT ALL OF US BLACK FOLKS COULDN'T BE PENNYWISE BARBERS. TOTAL FREEDOM COULD COME ONLY ONE WAY: SLAVERY HAD TO END.

EITHER VIOLENCE OR THE LAW WOULD BRING IT DOWN.

1800: RICHMOND, VIRGINIA

IF WE ORGANIZE, WE CAN SECURE OUR FREEDOM.

GABRIEL PROSSER WAS A SLAVE WHO WAS ENCOURAGED BY THE 1791 REVOLUTION IN HAITI, WHERE AFRICANS FREED THEMSELVES FROM FRENCH RULE. PROSSER DECIDED THAT THE SAME THING COULD HAPPEN IN VIRGINIA. HE WAS BETRAYED BY AN INFORMER AND HIS REVOLT NEVER MATERIALIZED.

WE COULD USE MORE NIGGERS LIKE YOU. I'LL SEE TO IT THAT YOU GET SPECIAL TREATMENT.

THANK YOU, SIR.

1800: PHILADELPHIA. A GROUP OF FREE BLACKS LED BY REVEREND ABSALOM JONES TRIED A DIFFERENT APPROACH.

THIS DOCUMENT I HAVE IN MY HAND IS A PETITION TO CONGRESS. IT CALLS FOR NEW LEGISLATION TO END THE SLAVE TRADE AND TO PUT AN END TO SLAVERY.

REJECTED

I DON'T EVEN NEED TO TELL YOU HOW CONGRESS VOTED ON THAT ONE.

BY THE BEGINNING OF THE NINETEENTH CENTURY, SLAVERY HAD EVOLVED INTO A SYSTEM DESIGNED TO KEEP THE MAJORITY OF BLACK FOLKS PSYCHOLOGICALLY AND ECONOMICALLY DEPENDENT ON THEIR MASTERS.

BUT SLAVERY COULDN'T STOP US FROM DREAMING OF BETTER DAYS.

MY LAND

HALF OF THE SLAVES IN THE SOUTH, AND ALMOST ALL OF THEM IN THE NORTH, LIVED ON SMALL FARMS, SO THE FARMHAND WAS THE MOST COMMONLY FOUND SLAVE.

STILL THOSE DREAMS WERE DEFERRED. FOR ALL PRACTICAL PURPOSES, THERE WERE FOUR TYPES OF SLAVES: THE FARMHAND, AND ON LARGE PLANTATIONS, THE HOUSE SLAVE, THE FIELD SLAVE, AND THE WORKSHOP SLAVE. EACH HAD WAYS OF DEALING WITH SLAVERY.

PTOO!

THO' IN SOME SITUATIONS THE FARMER AND FARMHANDS WORKED MORE AS PARTNERS THAN AS MASTER AND SLAVE.

USUALLY THERE WERE NO MORE THAN THREE FARMHANDS LIVING ON A FARM. TO THE FARMOWNER, THEY WERE BEASTS OF BURDEN LIKE A MULE OR AN OX.

AFTER YOU CHOP THOSE LOGS, I WANT YOU TO BALE THAT HAY.

YOU. YOU! YOU! ? ? ? ME?

LUCIUS, I NEED A HAND WITH THESE LOGS.

WHEN I FINISH, BOSS.

... AND UNENDING PHYSICAL ABUSE.

YET THROUGH THESE HARDSHIPS, FOLKWAYS FROM AFRICA HELPED CREATE AN AFRICAN AMERICAN CULTURE OF SURVIVAL.

WE USED MUSIC TO EASE OUR BURDEN.

MANY WHITE PEOPLE SAW THOSE FOLKWAYS AS HARMLESS RECREATION AND OFTEN EMULATED THE SLAVES.

WE TOLD STORIES FOR INSPIRATION, ENTERTAINMENT AND LESSONS ABOUT HOW TO SURVIVE.

LEMME TELL 'YA BOUT BR'ER RABBIT.

THAT THING SURE SOUNDS GOOD. WHAT DO YOU CALL IT, BOY?

A BANJO.

BUT WHAT THE FIELD SLAVES DID WAS FAR FROM HARMLESS RECREATION. IT WAS A DAILY **RE-CREATION** OF A CULTURE THAT PROTECTED THEM FROM BEING DESTROYED BY A RECKLESS AND RAPACIOUS NEW NATION.

AS A NEW NATION, AMERICA GOT THE URGE TO STRETCH ITS LEGS. MANY AMERICANS MOVED WESTWARD.

BUT IT WASN'T JUST THE "NATIVE" WHITE AMERICANS GOING WEST. THERE WERE NEW EUROPEAN IMMIGRANTS FROM GERMANY, SCOTLAND, AND IRELAND.

AND OF COURSE THERE WERE THE AFRICANS.

IN 1804, IF IT WASN'T FOR A MAN NAMED YORK, THE EXPEDITIONS OF LEWIS AND CLARK WOULD HAVE FLOPPED BIG TIME.

HE SERVED AS THEIR GUIDE,...

WE'LL FIND WATER OVER THOSE HILLS.

...HE SERVED AS THEIR SCOUT,...

...BUT HE ALSO SERVED AS THEIR SLAVE.

WHEN YOU FINISH WITH THE FOOD, GO CUT SOME FIREWOOD FOR US.

UNLIKE YORK, MARIE THÉRÈSE WAS NO FRONTIERSMAN.

SHE WAS A VISIONARY.

1799: LOUISIANA

WE MAY NOT ALL BE FREE, BUT THOSE OF US THAT ARE WILL LIVE LIKE HUMAN BEINGS.

BY 1803, MARIE THÉRÈSE HAD USED HER LIFE SAVINGS TO BRING HER VISION OF AN ALL-BLACK PLANTATION TO LIFE. IT WAS CALLED ISLE BREVELLE AND IT WAS 13,000 ACRES IN SIZE.

THOUGH THERE WAS LOTS OF WORK TO DO ON ISLE BREVELLE, THE LABOR WAS NOT FORCED, AND THERE WERE NO BRUTAL MASTERS TO DEAL WITH.

BUT FOR MOST BLACK PEOPLE IN THE EARLY 1800s, THE CLOSEST THING TO INDEPENDENCE WAS THE FEW HOURS OF SLEEP BETWEEN DAYS OF BACK-BREAKING SLAVING.

IN 1805, VIRGINIA PASSED A LAW REQUIRING FREED SLAVES TO LEAVE THE STATE AND FROM THE EARLY 1800s TO THE 1830s, MANY NORTHERN STATES TOOK THE RIGHT TO VOTE FROM PROPERTY-HOLDING BLACKS AND GAVE THAT RIGHT TO PROPERTYLESS WHITES. IN AN AGE THAT WAS SUPPOSED TO BE ENLIGHTENED TO THE IDEALS OF DEMOCRACY AND LIBERTY, IT SEEMED MORE AND MORE LIKE TIME WAS STANDING STILL FOR BLACK PEOPLE.

YET FOR ALL HIS 'ENLIGHTENMENT,' TROUBLE WAS ON THE HORIZON FOR OLD UNCLE SAM.

SINCE BRITAIN HAD THE MOST POWERFUL NAVY IN THE WORLD, IT CONTROLLED THE HIGH SEAS.

BY 1812, UNCLE SAM'S WESTWARD EXPANSION GOT HIM CAUGHT IN THE MIDDLE OF A WAR BETWEEN BRITAIN, SPAIN, AND FRANCE.

VOUS ÊTES UN CRETIN.

GO TO BLOODY HELL, YOU BLASTED FROG!

SORRY, YANK, BUT UNLESS YER DOCKIN' AT A BRITISH PORT, THIS IS AS FAR AS YOU CAN GO WITHOUT ME BLOWIN' YER SHIP OUT OF THE WATER.

INCIDENTS LIKE THOSE ENRAGED A GROUP OF MIDWESTERN CONGRESSIONAL REPRESENTATIVES, KNOWN AS THE **WAR HAWKS**.

WITH ALL DUE RESPECT, PRESIDENT MADISON, WE MUST RETALIATE AGAINST THE BRITISH.

YES, WE MUST NOT LET OURSELVES BE BULLIED ANY LONGER.

DEFEATING THIS BRITISH AND SPANISH ALLIANCE WILL HELP US ACQUIRE SPANISH FLORIDA AND HER VAST RESOURCES.

I SEE YOUR POINT. THE ONLY QUESTION IS, CAN WE WIN?

MEANWHILE, BACK IN THE SLAVE QUARTERS AND THE FREE BLACK COMMUNITIES, SOME BLACKS EMBARKED ON WHAT THEY BELIEVED WAS A PATH TO FREEDOM AND EQUALITY.

IF WE FIGHT WITH THE WHITE MAN, I'M SURE HE WILL ABOLISH SLAVERY THIS TIME.

THAT WHITE MAN AIN'T GONNA FREE ALL OF US. MAYBE HE'LL FREE A FEW OF US FOR THE LOOKS O' THINGS, BUT THE REST OF US HE'S GONNA USE LIKE HE ALWAYS DO.

YOU CAN MISS THIS OPPORTUNITY IF YOU WANT, BUT I'M GONNA FIGHT AND GET MY FREEDOM.

SOME OF US NEVER LEARN.

ONE IN SIX OF ALL SEAMEN IN THE WAR OF 1812 WAS BLACK.

THIS WAS A HARD AND BRUTAL WAR FOR AMERICA.

IN 1814, THE BRITISH BURNED WASHINGTON, D.C., TO THE GROUND. A GROUP OF 2,500 PHILADELPHIA BLACKS LED BY JAMES FORTEN, RICHARD ALLEN, AND ABSALOM JONES RESPONDED WITH PATRIOTISM AND HUMANITY BY HELPING TO REBUILD WASHINGTON.

STILL DIDN'T CHANGE MUCH.

I'D LIKE TO THANK YOU, GENTLEMEN FOR HELPING AMERICA. WHAT CAN WE DO TO SHOW OUR GRATITUDE?

YOU CAN FREE MY BRETHREN WHO STILL LANGUISH IN SLAVERY.

THAT WASN'T QUITE WHAT I HAD IN MIND.

YET MANY BLACK PEOPLE STILL FELT THAT DEMONSTRATIONS OF BRAVERY AND INTEGRITY WOULD EVENTUALLY WIN THE WHITE MAN OVER.

IN 1815, AN ALL-BLACK BATTALION IN NEW ORLEANS, KNOWN AS THE FREE MEN OF COLOR, THOUGHT THEIR HEROISM WOULD TRANSLATE INTO JUSTICE AND FREEDOM FOR ALL.

WITH THE SPIRIT OF REBELLION IN THEIR SOULS THEY FOUGHT HARD IN WHAT WOULD BE THE LAST BATTLE OF THE WAR OF 1812.

WHEN THE GUNSMOKE CLEARED, MORE THAN 2,000 BRITISH TROOPS WERE DEAD, AND THE FREE MEN OF COLOR WERE READY TO REAP THE REWARDS OF THEIR VICTORY.
REWARD NEVER CAME. IN FACT, THEY WERE NOT EVEN ALLOWED TO MARCH IN THE ANNUAL PARADES COMMEMORATING THE VICTORY.

THERE WAS ONE WEALTHY FREE BLACK SAILOR NAMED PAUL CUFFE, WHO COULD NO LONGER TOLERATE PAYING THE COSTS OF BEING AN AMERICAN WITHOUT RECEIVING ANY OF THE BENEFITS.

1780: BOSTON

AS FREE AFRICAN MEN AND WOMEN, WHY SHOULD WE PAY TAXES WHEN WE CANNOT EVEN VOTE?

BY 1814, CUFFE HAD TRAVELED THE WORLD, AND HIS IDEAS HAD EVOLVED OVER TIME.

IF THERE'S NO JUSTICE IN AMERICA, MAYBE WE CAN HAVE IT IN AFRICA.

65

WITH A LITTLE HELP FROM SUCCESSFUL BLACK PHILADELPHIA SHIPBUILDER JAMES FORTEN, A PLAN TO TRANSPORT A FEW BLACKS TO AFRICA WAS CONCEIVED.

A FEW DAYS LATER IN PHILADELPHIA, THE FREE AFRICAN SOCIETY DEBATED CUFFE'S PLAN:

THIS IS THE SAME ARGUMENT WE HAD WITH OUR BROTHERS IN RHODE ISLAND OVER TWENTY YEARS AGO. BY GOING TO AFRICA, WE ABANDON OUR SLAVE SISTERS AND BROTHERS IN THIS LAND.

PERHAPS, BUT IF WE STAY HERE THE WHITE MAN WILL EITHER KILL US OR DRIVE US INSANE.

BROTHER ALLEN, DON'T BUST YOUR BLOOMERS. BROTHER CUFFE ONLY HAS ONE SHIP AND ALL OF US CAN'T FIT IN IT.

IT MAY BE ONLY ONE BOAT NOW, BUT MARK MY WORDS, THIS TRIP IS GOING TO HAVE CONSEQUENCES.

IN 1815, CUFFE AND 38 OTHER FREE BLACK MEN AND WOMEN SET SAIL FOR THE AFRICAN NATION OF SIERRA LEONE.

ANCHORS AWEIGH!

WHILE CUFFE TRAVELLED TO THE CONTINENT OF HIS LOST ANCESTRAL HOME, SOME WHITES LOOKED FOR MORE NEW LAND TO CONQUER.

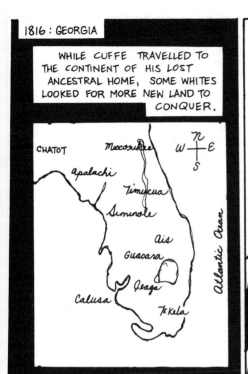

MY GOOD MEN, AS YOU KNOW, ONE OF THE AIMS OF THE WAR OF 1812 WAS TO EXPAND AMERICAN SOVEREIGNTY.

I BEG YOUR PARDON, SIR?

HE MEANS WE FOUGHT TO ACQUIRE MORE LAND.

WELL, OUR PLANS ARE NOW COMING TO FRUITION. THE BRITISH AND THE SPANISH HAVE ABANDONED A FORTRESS IN NORTHERN FLORIDA.

EXCELLENT. FLORIDA WILL SOON BE OURS.

IT WILL NOT BE QUITE SO EASY. RUNAWAY SLAVES AND INDIANS HAVE TAKEN OVER THE FORTRESS. ONCE WE SUBDUE THEM, **THEN** FLORIDA WILL BE OURS.

FOR MORE THAN 80 YEARS, FLORIDA HAD SERVED AS A PLACE OF REFUGE FOR RUNAWAY SLAVES AND NATIVE AMERICANS WHO TOGETHER HAD NEGOTIATED TREATIES WITH BOTH THE SPANISH AND THE BRITISH. BY 1816, FLORIDA WAS ON ITS WAY TO BECOMING A NATION RUN BY BLACKS AND NATIVE AMERICANS.

THE FORTRESS THEY ACQUIRED WAS RENAMED **FORT NEGRO**.

IN JULY 1816, AMERICA PREPARED TO ATTACK THE FORT.

LED BY A FORMER SLAVE NAMED GARSON, THE AFRICAN-NATIVE AMERICAN ALLIANCE REPELLED THE FIRST AMERICAN ATTACK.

BUT ULTIMATELY THE FIREPOWER OF THE AMERICAN MILITARY OVERWHELMED THE RESISTANCE AND FORT NEGRO WAS DESTROYED. IN YEARS TO COME, IN FIERCE BATTLES KNOWN AS THE SEMINOLE WARS, THE BLACK AND NATIVE AMERICAN ALLIANCE WOULD BE DEFEATED AND ALL OF FLORIDA WOULD BE CONQUERED BY AMERICA.

YET IN SPITE OF THE DESTRUCTION AT FORT NEGRO AND THE CONTINUED PROLIFERATION OF WHITE RACISM, THERE WERE DECENT WHITE PEOPLE WHO TRULY WANTED JUSTICE. ONE OF THEM WAS GEORGE BOXLEY.

1816: SPOTSYLVANIA, PENNSYLVANIA

IN A FEW WEEKS, WE SHALL FREE ALL THE SLAVES IN SPOTSYLVANIA.

UNFORTUNATELY, BOXLEY'S PLANS WERE DISCOVERED. BOXLEY ESCAPED BUT SIX SLAVES WERE HANGED.

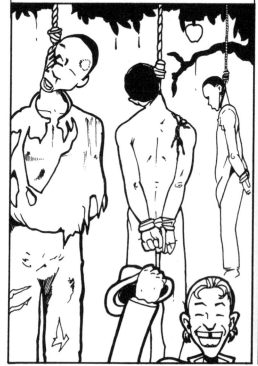

1816: PHILADELPHIA

ACROSS THE STATE, FREE BLACKS PUSHED ON.

THE AFRICAN METHODIST EPISCOPAL CHURCH, THE FIRST NATIONAL CHURCH OF AFRICAN PEOPLE IN AMERICA, IS HEREBY BROUGHT INTO EXISTENCE. AND WE ELECT BROTHER RICHARD ALLEN AS OUR FIRST BISHOP!

70

71

THE GROWTH OF THE AMERICAN COLONIZATION SOCIETY SPARKED DEBATE IN THE FREE BLACK COMMUNITY. ONE OF ITS MOST OUTSPOKEN OPPONENTS WAS JAMES FORTEN, WHO HAD ASSISTED PAUL CUFFE.

WE CANNOT LET WHITE PEOPLE DETERMINE WHERE AND HOW WE SHOULD LIVE. THIS SOCIETY IS A VEILED ATTEMPT TO DO JUST THAT.

BUT JUST TWO YEARS AGO, YOU SUPPORTED YOUR FRIEND MR. CUFFE IN HIS ENDEAVOR. HAD YOU NOT DONE THAT, THE SEED OF THIS IDEA TO DEPORT US WOULD HAVE NEVER BEEN SOWN.

IT IS TRUE THAT I SUPPORTED BROTHER CUFFE, AND I STILL SUPPORT HIM. I AM NOT AGAINST SOME OF OUR PEOPLE MIGRATING TO AFRICA. BUT IT MUST BE VOLUNTARY. OUR PEOPLE HAVE BLED AND DIED IN AND FOR THIS LAND. EACH MUST BE FREE TO DECIDE WHERE TO LIVE.

IN 1819, THE UNITED STATES FACED A DILEMMA. ITS EVEN BALANCE — TWENTY-TWO SENATORS FROM FREE STATES, AND TWENTY-TWO FROM SLAVE STATES — WAS NEARLY UPSET WHEN MISSOURI PETITIONED CONGRESS FOR STATEHOOD AS A SLAVEHOLDING STATE. SINCE MISSOURI FELL OUTSIDE OF THE BOUNDARIES OF THE NORTHWEST ORDINANCE OF 1787, IT WASN'T CLEAR WHAT TO DO.

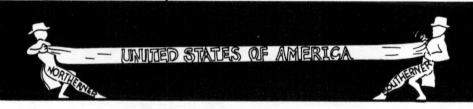

THE MISSOURI COMPROMISE IN 1820 ADMITTED MISSOURI AS A SLAVE STATE, AND MAINE AS A NON-SLAVE STATE, AND ALSO DREW A LINE AT 36' 30 LATITUDE ACROSS THE LOUISIANA TERRITORY. WITH THE EXCEPTION OF MISSOURI, SLAVERY WAS OUTLAWED IN ALL AREAS NORTH OF THAT LINE.
THAT COMPROMISE AVERTED A CRISIS, BUT ALSO TORE AT THE FABRIC OF THE UNION.

MEANWHILE, A BLACK MAN IN CHARLESTON, SOUTH CAROLINA, PREPARED TO TAKE AN UNCOMPROMISING STAND AGAINST SLAVERY.

LIKE PAUL CUFFE AND JAMES FORTEN, DENMARK VESEY WAS A WELL-OFF FREE MAN. AS A CARPENTER HE ACHIEVED A LEVEL OF WEALTH THAT SURPASSED THAT OF MANY WHITES IN SOUTH CAROLINA.

I CANNOT LET THIS GO ON ANY LONGER.

PAP!

VESEY BEGAN PLANNING A REBELLION IN CHARLESTON. HE USED THE AME CHURCH IN CHARLESTON AS ONE OF HIS MEETING PLACES.

WE CAN AND WILL OVERTHROW THE WHITE MAN!

ONE DAY SOON YOU'LL HAVE YOUR REVENGE.

73

AND IN THE SUMMER OF 1822, THEY WERE READY.

FOR YEARS VESEY WORKED IN THE COMMUNITIES OF FREE BLACKS AND SLAVES TO PLAN HIS REVOLT.

UNFORTUNATELY, VESEY'S PLANS WERE BETRAYED BY A BLACK INFORMANT.

GOOD WORK, BOY, HERE ARE YOUR FREE PAPERS JUST LIKE I PROMISED.

THANKS

BECAUSE OF THE BETRAYAL, THE WHITE COMMUNITY IN CHARLESTON PREEMPTED THE REVOLT BY ARRESTING 139 SLAVES. VESEY AND 46 OTHERS WERE HANGED.

AS WAS ALWAYS THE CASE AFTER SLAVE REVOLTS, LIFE FOR BLACK PEOPLE— WHETHER FREE OR SLAVE— GREW HARSHER.

NOBODY SAID FREEDOM CAME EASY.

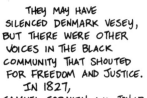

They may have silenced Denmark Vesey, but there were other voices in the black community that shouted for freedom and justice.

In 1827, Samuel Cornish and John B. Russworm, one of the first black college graduates in the U.S., founded FREEDOM'S JOURNAL in New York City.

And in 1829, a 44-year-old free black man published a pamphlet that challenged the American social order.

DAVID WALKER'S APPEAL

LISTEN TO THIS.

"...AMERICA IS MORE OUR COUNTRY THAN IT IS THE WHITES'— WE HAVE ENRICHED IT WITH OUR BLOOD AND TEARS. THE GREATEST RICHES IN ALL AMERICA HAVE ARISEN FROM OUR BLOOD AND TEARS: AND THEY WILL DRIVE US FROM OUR PROPERTY AND HOMES, WHICH WE HAVE EARNED WITH BLOOD."

GET RID OF THE NIGGERS.

KILL THE NIGGERS, THEY'RE TAKIN' OUR JOBS!

Walker's words were a direct response to mob violence that occurred in Cincinnati, Ohio, in August 1829

76

AS NEWS OF NAT TURNER SPREAD, THE WHITE SOUTHERN PLANTERS RESPONDED WITH THEIR OWN SPECIAL BRAND OF SOUTHERN BRUTALITY

THE LEADERS OF VIRGINIA LEFT NO STONE UNTURNED UNTIL NAT TURNER WAS CAPTURED. ON OCTOBER 31, TURNER WAS APPREHENDED BY THE VIRGINIA AUTHORITIES.

ON NOVEMBER 11, 1831, NAT TURNER ACCEPTED HIS EXECUTION CALMLY.

IT'S IN GOD'S HANDS NOW.

MEANWHILE, ALTHEIA TURNER AND JANE MINOR, BOTH FREE BLACKS, USED THEIR MONEY TO BUY THE FREEDOM OF SLAVES THROUGHOUT THE SOUTH.

AT THE SAME TIME, FREE BLACKS IN NEW YORK LIKE DAVID RUGGLES WORKED TO UNDERMINE SLAVERY BY SECURING FREEDOM FOR RUNAWAY SLAVES. TWO ESCAPEES HE AIDED WERE FREDERICK DOUGLASS AND HIS WIFE ANNA MURRAY.

DON'T FRET, YOU'RE WITH FRIENDS NOW.

SMALL BUT GROWING GROUPS OF WHITES STOOD UP AGAINST SLAVERY.
SOME WERE MOTIVATED BY THE RELIGIOUS REVIVALS OF THE EARLY 1830s.

IN 1833, A WHITE MAN BY THE NAME OF WILLIAM LLOYD GARRISON FORMED THE AMERICAN ANTI-SLAVERY SOCIETY. WITH THE HELP OF EDUCATED BLACK ABOLITIONISTS LIKE PETER WILLIAMS JR., GARRISON ORGANIZED ABOLITIONISTS OF BOTH RACES.
THE SOCIETY'S STRATEGY WAS TO GAIN WHITE SUPPORT BY SPONSORING LECTURES THROUGHOUT THE COUNTRY.

SLAVERY MUST BE ABOLISHED. IT IS IMMORAL FOR HUMANS TO ENSLAVE ONE ANOTHER.

HOLY BIBLE

SLAVERY SHALL DOOM ALL OF US TO HELL.

THE SOCIETY FORMALLY ORGANIZED WHITE PEOPLE AGAINST SLAVERY, BUT SOME BLACKS HAD QUESTIONS.

FREEDOM IS IN THE AIR, BROTHER. NOW EVEN WHITE FOLKS ARE TALKIN' 'BOUT ENDIN' SLAVERY.

MAYBE SO, BUT THOSE WHITE FOLKS DON'T OWN NO SLAVES. SO HOW ARE THEY GONNA END IT?

SKEPTICISM ABOUT THE ANTI-SLAVERY SOCIETY WAS NOT UNFOUNDED.
BLACK MEN IN THE ORGANIZATION HAD LIMITED DECISION-MAKING POWERS, WHILE BLACK WOMEN WERE KEPT OUT OF POWER COMPLETELY
STILL, MANY FREE BLACKS JOINED THE SOCIETY.

WHILE ORGANIZATIONS LIKE THE AMERICAN ANTI-SLAVE SOCIETY AND THE NATIONAL COLORED CONVENTION LOOKED FOR WAYS TO TRANSFORM AMERICAN DEMOCRACY, BLACK INVENTORS LOOKED FOR WAYS TO TRANSFORM AMERICAN TECHNOLOGY.

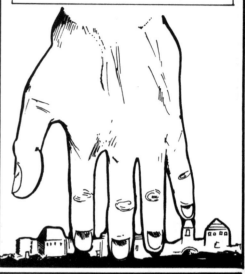

IN 1834, CYRUS McCORMICK INVENTED THE REAPER — A MACHINE THAT WOULD REVOLUTIONIZE FARMING.

OF COURSE THE INVENTION WOULD NOT HAVE BEEN POSSIBLE WITHOUT THE EFFORTS OF HIS SLAVE JOE ANDERSON.

 ANOTHER SLAVE INVENTOR WHO HAD BETTER LUCK WAS HENRY BLAIR, WHO RECEIVED A PATENT FOR A CORN PLANTER THE SAME YEAR AS McCORMICK'S REAPER APPEARED.

BUT SLAVE INVENTIONS LIKE THOSE TOOK A BACKSEAT TO THE GREATEST INVENTION OF ALL, THE UNDERGROUND RAILROAD.

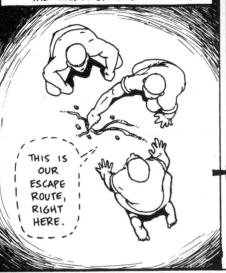

THIS IS OUR ESCAPE ROUTE, RIGHT HERE.

THE UNDERGROUND RAILROAD ESTABLISHED A NETWORK OF SECRET MEETING PLACES WHERE ESCAPING SLAVES COULD FIND REFUGE AND BE LED TO FREEDOM.
IT GREATLY INCREASED THE NUMBER OF SUCCESSFUL ESCAPES FROM SLAVERY.
FREE NORTHERN BLACKS LIKE WILLIAM STILL IN PHILADELPHIA AND DAVID RUGGLES IN NEW YORK FORMED VIGILANCE COMMITTEES TO PROVIDE SOME OF THE INITIAL HIDING PLACES AND OFTEN ARMED PROTECTION AGAINST FEDERAL SLAVE-CATCHERS. WITH THEIR HELP THE UNDERGROUND RAILROAD BEGAN TO FLOURISH IN THE MID-1830s.

ALSO IN THE 1830s, TWO EVENTS OUTSIDE AMERICA'S BORDERS GAVE THE BURGEONING FREEDOM MOVEMENT ANOTHER SHOT IN THE ARM.

1833: LONDON, ENGLAND

FROM THIS DAY FORWARD THE ENGLISH PARLIAMENT HEREBY ABOLISHES SLAVERY IN ALL OF HER COLONIES.

SOMEWHERE IN THE ATLANTIC, ANOTHER SIGNIFICANT EVENT BEGAN TO UNFOLD.

IN 1839, A GROUP OF ENSLAVED AFRICANS ON A SPANISH SLAVE SHIP, THE AMISTAD, WHICH SAILED FROM HAVANA, CUBA, KILLED THE CAPTAIN AND GAINED CONTROL OF THE SHIP. AFTER SAILING FOR TWO MONTHS THEY WERE CAPTURED OFF OF THE COAST OF LONG ISLAND, AND PUT IN A NEW HAVEN, CONNECTICUT, JAIL. IT WAS DECIDED THAT SINCE THE KILLING OCCURRED AT SEA, THE AFRICANS, LED BY A MAN NAMED CINQUE, COULD NOT BE CHARGED WITH MURDER.

TWO YEARS AND TWO COURT CASES LATER, IT WAS UP TO THE SUPREME COURT TO DECIDE WHAT TO DO.

THE LAW CLEARLY STATES THAT THE IMPORTATION OF NEGROES WAS MADE ILLEGAL IN 1808. FOR THAT REASON THE COURT HAS NO OTHER ALTERNATIVE THAN TO SET CINQUE AND HIS ASSOCIATES FREE.

AFTER THAT VERDICT WE THOUGHT WE SAW FREEDOM ON THE HORIZON, BUT WE WOULD FIND OUT PRETTY SOON THAT IT WAS ONLY A MIRAGE.

AUG. 1, 1842: PHILADELPHIA, PENNSYLVANIA. A FESTIVE CROWD CELEBRATES THE NINTH ANNIVERSARY OF THE BRITISH ABOLITION OF SLAVERY.

GREGSMITH

IF THEY CAN DO THAT TO THOSE OF US WHO ARE FREE, WHO KNOWS WHAT THEY CAN DO TO US STILL IN SLAVERY?

THAT ANTI-SLAVERY SOCIETY'S BEEN WORKING DARN NEAR TEN YEARS AND AIN'T GOT NOTHIN' TO SHOW FOR IT.

YOU CAN'T BE SO CONTRARY. THOSE ABOLITIONISTS ARE DOIN' THE BEST THEY CAN.

IN 1842, BUTTRESSED BY A GROWING SENSE OF DISILLUSIONMENT AND MILITANCY, THE NATIONAL COLORED CONVENTION RESUMED IN ROCHESTER AFTER AN EIGHT-YEAR HIATUS.

THE CONVENTION HAD MORE THAN SEVENTY DELEGATES FROM MORE THAN TWELVE STATES. AMONG THE ATTENDEES WERE INFLUENTIAL YOUNG BLACK ABOLITIONISTS LIKE WILLIAM WELLS BROWN, WILLIAM STILL, AND FREDERICK DOUGLASS.

IT'S GOOD TO SEE YOU HERE, BROTHERS.

THOUGH THERE WERE MANY IMPORTANT MEN AT THE CONVENTION, A 27-YEAR-OLD FORMER SLAVE, REVEREND HENRY HIGHLAND GARNET, COMMANDED THE GREATEST PRESENCE.

IN 1822 DENMARK VESEY FORMED A PLAN FOR THE LIBERATION OF HIS FELLOW MEN.

IN THE WHOLE HISTORY OF HUMAN EFFORTS TO OVERTHROW SLAVERY, A MORE COMPLICATED AND TREMENDOUS PLAN WAS NEVER FORMED.

HE WAS BETRAYED BY THE TREACHERY OF HIS OWN PEOPLE, AND DIED A MARTYR TO FREEDOM.... BRETHREN ARISE, ARISE !

STRIKE FOR YOUR LIVES AND LIBERTIES.

NOW IS THE DAY AND THE HOUR. LET EVERY SLAVE THROUGHOUT THE LAND DO THIS AND THE DAYS OF SLAVERY ARE NUMBERED.

THOUGH GARNET SHOCKED MANY OF THE CONVENTIONEERS, MANY AGREED WITH HIM.

HE'S GONE MAD.

HE HAS A POINT.

WHEN THE CONVENTIONEERS VOTED ON WHETHER OR NOT TO ADOPT GARNET'S MESSAGE AS A RESOLUTION, IT WAS DEFEATED BY A MARGIN OF ONE VOTE.

NONETHELESS, HENRY HIGHLAND GARNET HAD MADE HIS POINT.

1843 : NEW YORK CITY

WHILE SOME PEOPLE WERE STEPPING UP THEIR EFFORTS TO END AMERICAN SLAVERY, SOME WHITE PEOPLE CHOSE TO RIDICULE BLACKS AND THEIR CULTURE.

DAN EMMETT AND HIS FRIENDS FORMED THE VIRGINIA MINSTRELS, A GROUP OF WHITE MEN WHO PORTRAYED BLACK PEOPLE AS SIMPLE AND HAPPY TO BE SLAVES.

BEFORE LONG THE MINSTREL SHOW BECAME A NATIONAL PHENOMENON.

AND TO THIS DAY SOME AMERICANS, BOTH BLACK AND WHITE, CONTINUE TO STEREOTYPE AND OVERSIMPLIFY BLACK PEOPLE FOR FUN AND PROFIT.

BUT WHILE THE MYTH OF THE BLACK SIMPLETON SPREAD, IT COULD NOT OUTPACE BLACK DIGNITY. NO ONE PERSONIFIED THAT DIGNITY MORE POWERFULLY THAN AN ESCAPED SLAVE NAMED FREDERICK DOUGLASS.

BY 1845, DOUGLASS WAS ONE OF THE MOST FAMOUS MEMBERS OF THE AMERICAN ANTI-SLAVERY SOCIETY.

HE HELD AUDIENCES CAPTIVE WHEN HE SPOKE OF HIS TIME IN SLAVERY.

THE AMERICAN ANTI-SLAVERY SOCIETY PRESENTS: FREDERICK DOUGLASS

BUT AS HE GREW INTELLECTUALLY, HE WANTED TO HELP PLAN THE STRATEGIES OF THE ORGANIZATION.

WILLIAM, I FEEL IT IS TIME FOR US TO EXPLORE THE POLITICAL APPROACH TO ABOLITION AS WELL AS THE MORAL APPROACH.

FREDERICK, ALL YOU NEED TO DO IS TALK ABOUT SLAVERY.

LET ME WORRY ABOUT ABOLISHING IT.

The North Star

BY 1847, DOUGLASS DECIDED TO STRIKE OUT ON HIS OWN AND PRESENT HIS IDEAS ABOUT ENDING SLAVERY AND REALIZING DEMOCRACY IN AMERICA.

HIS FIRST IDEA WAS TO PUBLISH A NEWSPAPER, THE NORTH STAR, WITH A PROUD BLACK DOCTOR FROM PITTSBURGH NAMED MARTIN DELANY.

87

ANOTHER IMAGINATIVE ESCAPE WAS MADE IN 1848 BY THE MARRIED COUPLE WILLIAM AND ELLEN CRAFT. ELLEN DISGUISED HERSELF AS AN INVALID WHITE MALE PLANTER TRAVELING FROM MARYLAND TO OHIO WITH WILLIAM AS HER SLAVE. THEY ALSO BECAME PART OF THE ABOLITIONIST LECTURE CIRCUIT.

BUT THE PERSON WHO BEST EXEMPLIFIED THE SPIRIT OF THE UNDERGROUND RAILROAD WAS HARRIET TUBMAN.

IN 1849, WHEN SHE LEARNED THAT SHE WAS GOING TO BE SOLD FURTHER SOUTH, SHE TOLD HER HUSBAND, A FREE BLACK NAMED JOHN:

TUBMAN DECIDED TO ESCAPE FROM SLAVERY WITHOUT HER HUSBAND'S SUPPORT.

THEY'RE GONNA SELL ME, JOHN. WE GOTTA GET AWAY FROM HERE BEFORE THEY SEPARATE US.

WOMAN, STOP YO' FUSSIN'. I AIN'T NO SLAVE AND THEY AIN'T SELLIN' NO BODY.

BUT SHE LOVED HER HUSBAND SO MUCH SHE DECIDED TO RETURN TO DORCHESTER COUNTY, MARYLAND, TO CONVINCE HIM TO COME BACK TO PHILADELPHIA WITH HER.

SHE WAS A TRUE SLAVE TO LOVE 'CAUSE THE JOURNEY BACK WAS MORE DANGEROUS THAN THE ESCAPE ITSELF. SOMEHOW SHE MADE IT.

WHEN SHE DISCOVERED THAT HE HAD TAKEN UP WITH ANOTHER WOMAN AND DID NOT WANT TO LEAVE, HARRIET WAS HEARTBROKEN.

BUT INSTEAD OF DESPAIRING, SHE DEDICATED HERSELF TO THE UNDERGROUND RAILROAD.

THIS RIVER LEADS TO FREEDOM.

AT THE SAME TIME THAT THE UNDERGROUND RAILROAD WAS SENDING THOUSANDS OF RUNAWAY SLAVES NORTH, A NEW FIND IN THE TERRITORY OF CALIFORNIA DRAMATICALLY ALTERED THE AMERICAN LANDSCAPE.

IT'S GOLD!

ON JANUARY 24, 1848, JAMES MARSHALL AND JOHN A. SUTTER STRUCK GOLD IN CALIFORNIA AND AMERICANS SURGED WEST AT A RECORD PACE, A MIGRATION LATER CALLED THE GOLD RUSH.

ALVIN COFFEY WAS ONE OF THE FEW BLACK PEOPLE WHO PROFITED FROM THE CALIFORNIA GOLD RUSH.

IN 1849 COFFEY WAS TAKEN FROM ST. LOUIS TO CALIFORNIA BY HIS MASTER. WORKING THE GOLD MINES AT NIGHT FOR HIMSELF, HE SOON AMASSED FIVE THOUSAND DOLLARS WORTH OF GOLD AND PLANNED TO BUY HIS FAMILY'S FREEDOM.

WHEN COFFEY'S OWNER FOUND OUT ABOUT COFFEY'S PERSONAL STASH, HE CONFISCATED IT AND SOLD COFFEY TO ANOTHER OWNER.

INCREDIBLY, COFFEY WAS ABLE TO CONVINCE HIS NEW OWNER THAT HE COULD MAKE THE OWNER A RICH MAN IF COFFEY WERE ALLOWED TO WORK IN THE MINES TO PURCHASE HIS FAMILY'S FREEDOM.

COFFEY SUCCEEDED IN FREEING HIS FAMILY, AND IN YEARS TO COME THE COFFEY FAMILY LIVED AND PROSPERED IN TEHAMA COUNTY, CALIFORNIA.

1850: WASHINGTON, D.C.

OF COURSE, THE WESTWARD EXPANSION HAD OTHER CONSEQUENCES...

WE CAME OUT HERE TO FORM OUR OWN STATE, WITH OUR OWN RULES, AND AIN'T NO MONEY-GRUBBIN YANKEES GONNA STOP US.

IF IT'S DEATH YOU WANT, THEN IT'S DEATH YOU'LL GET...

GENTLEMEN! GENTLEMEN! I'M SURE WE CAN COME TO AN AGREEMENT.

WITH THE UNION IN JEOPARDY, PRESIDENT ZACHARY TAYLOR SIGNED THE COMPROMISE OF 1850, WHICH ABOLISHED THE SLAVE TRADE IN WASHINGTON, D.C., AND ALLOWED CALIFORNIA TO BE ADMITTED TO THE UNION AS A FREE STATE, BUT WHICH ALSO GAVE SOUTHERNERS MORE POWER TO RECAPTURE RUNAWAY SLAVES.

THIS FUGITIVE SLAVE LAW IS AN OUTRAGE. IF THE GOVERNMENT KEEPS CAVING IN TO THESE SOUTHERNERS, THE WHOLE COUNTRY WILL COME APART.

COMPROMISE, HA! NEXT THING YOU KNOW, THEM YANKEES'LL BE TELLIN' US HOW TO RUN OUR OWN STATES.

SOON AFTER, IN PHILADELPHIA IN 1851, THE COLORED AMERICAN INSTITUTE FOR THE PROMOTION OF THE MECHANIC ARTS AND SCIENCES HELD AN EXHIBITION TO DEMONSTRATE TECHNICAL ACCOMPLISHMENTS OF BLACK PEOPLE.

THESE THINGS HERE PROVE COLORED FOLKS CAN DO ANYTHING WHITE FOLKS CAN.

AND FEARLESS BLACK VOICES CONTINUED TO RING OUT. IN 1851, ONE OF THOSE VOICES BELONGED TO SOJOURNER TRUTH.

TRUTH WAS BORN INTO SLAVERY AS ISABELLA AROUND 1799. SHE CHANGED HER NAME TO SOJOURNER TRUTH IN 1843.

WHEN I LEFT THE HOUSE OF BONDAGE, I WASN'T GOING TO KEEP NOTHIN' OF SLAVERY ON ME. THE LORD GAVE ME THE NAME <u>SOJOURNER</u> BECAUSE I WAS TO TRAVEL UP AND DOWN THE LAND. LATER ON I TOLD HIM I WANTED A SECOND NAME CAUSE EVERYBODY GOT TWO NAMES. THEN HE GAVE ME <u>TRUTH</u> 'CAUSE I WAS SUPPOSED TO PROCLAIM THE TRUTH WHEREVER I WAS.

MAKING IT PLAIN AS PLAIN COULD BE, SOJOURNER CONNECTED WITH AUDIENCES WHEREVER SHE SPOKE.

NOW, I KNOW I CAN'T READ A BOOK, BUT I SURE CAN READ PEOPLE.

THE WOMAN SHOULD BE ALLOWED TO VOTE. AFTER ALL, SHE DOES AT LEAST HALF THE WORK IN THE LAND, AND FAIR IS FAIR.

OLD WOMAN, DO YOU THINK ALL YOUR TALK ABOUT SLAVERY DOES ANY GOOD? DO YOU THINK PEOPLE CARE ABOUT WHAT YOU SAY? WHY, I DON'T CARE ANY MORE FOR YOUR TALK THAN I DO FOR THE BITE OF A FLEA.

PERHAPS NOT, BUT THE GOOD LORD WILLING, I'LL KEEP YOU SCRATCHING.

ALSO IN 1851, AS SOJOURNER TRUTH WAS LECTURING AS AN ABOLITIONIST, WILLIAM NELL WROTE THE FIRST BLACK HISTORY BOOK, ENTITLED **THE SERVICES COLORED AMERICANS IN THE WARS OF 1776 AND 1812**.

AND IN 1851, A MARYLAND SLAVEOWNER NAMED EDWARD GORSUCH WENT TO PENNSYLVANIA TO FIND FOUR BLACK MEN WHO HAD ESCAPED FROM HIM TWO YEARS EARLIER. IN PHILADELPHIA, HE OBTAINED THE PROPER FEDERAL WARRANTS SPECIFIED BY THE FUGITIVE SLAVE ACT OF 1850. WITH A GROUP OF SEVEN OTHER MEN, INCLUDING HIS SON AND A UNITED STATES DEPUTY MARSHAL, HE SET OUT FOR CHRISTIANA, PENNSYLVANIA, A PLACE WHERE AN INFORMER TOLD HIM THE FUGITIVES COULD BE FOUND.

UNKNOWN TO THE WOULD-BE SLAVE CATCHERS, WILLIAM STILL'S PHILADELPHIA VIGILANCE COMMITTEE HAD A SPY WORKING NEAR THE FEDERAL OFFICE. SO THE ESCAPEES WERE PREPARED.

LED BY ONE OF THEIR OWN, WILLIAM PARKER, AND AIDED BY BLACK AND WHITE LOCALS, THE FUGITIVES READIED THEMSELVES.

U.S. FEDERAL OFFICE

THE VICTORY OVER THE SLAVE CATCHERS WAS SHORT-LIVED. WILLIAM PARKER NEEDED THE HELP OF FREDERICK DOUGLASS TO ESCAPE TO CANADA. LATER, SEVERAL BLACKS WHO WERE NOT INVOLVED IN AIDING PARKER AND TWO WHITES WHO REFUSED TO AID THE SLAVE CATCHERS WERE TRIED FOR TREASON.

THEY WERE REPRESENTED BY THADDEUS STEVENS, A WHITE NORTHERNER AND ABOLITIONIST. THEY WERE ACQUITTED IN TWENTY MINUTES. STEVENS WOULD GO ON TO BECOME AN INDEFATIGABLE ALLY OF BLACK PEOPLE IN THE U.S. CONGRESS.

THIS IS BUT A SMALL VICTORY IN THE WAR FOR FREEDOM.

INDEPENDENCE DAY, 1852: ROCHESTER, N.Y. FREDERICK DOUGLASS ADDRESSES A CROWD.

WHAT TO THE AMERICAN SLAVE IS YOUR FOURTH OF JULY? I ANSWER, A DAY THAT REVEALS TO HIM MORE THAN ALL OTHER DAYS OF THE YEAR, THE GROSS INJUSTICE AND CRUELTY TO WHICH HE IS THE CONSTANT VICTIM. TO HIM YOUR CELEBRATION IS A SHAM; YOUR BOASTED LIBERTY AN UNHOLY LICENSE; YOUR NATIONAL GREATNESS, SWELLING VANITY; YOUR SOUNDS OF REJOICING ARE EMPTY AND HEARTLESS;... YOUR SHOUTS OF LIBERTY AND EQUALITY HOLLOW MOCKERY;... A THIN VEIL TO COVER UP CRIMES WHICH WOULD DISGRACE A NATION OF SAVAGES. THERE IS NOT A NATION ON THE EARTH GUILTY OF PRACTICES MORE SHOCKING AND BLOODY THAN ARE THE PEOPLE OF THESE UNITED STATES AT THIS VERY HOUR.... LAY YOUR FACTS BY THE SIDE OF THE EVERYDAY PRACTICES OF THIS NATION, AND YOU WILL SAY WITH ME THAT FOR REVOLTING BARBARITY AND SHAMELESS HYPOCRISY, AMERICA REIGNS WITHOUT A RIVAL.

DESPITE THE FRUSTRATION AND ANGER EVIDENT IN HIS INDEPENDENCE DAY SPEECH, DOUGLASS STILL BELIEVED GREATLY IN AMERICA. IN 1853, HE MET WITH HARRIET BEECHER STOWE, THE AUTHOR OF THE CLASSIC ANTI-SLAVERY NOVEL UNCLE TOM'S CABIN.

MY PROJECT WILL PERMANENTLY CONTRIBUTE TO THE IMPROVEMENT AND ELEVATION OF THE FREE COLORED PEOPLE IN THE UNITED STATES.

BUT ANOTHER GROUP OF BLACKS, INCLUDING DOUGLASS'S FORMER PUBLISHING PARTNER MARTIN DELANY, AND AN ACTIVIST NAMED H. FORD DOUGLASS, SAW ABSOLUTELY NO HOPE FOR BLACK PEOPLE IN AMERICA, ESPECIALLY AFTER CONGRESS PASSED THE CONTROVERSIAL KANSAS-NEBRASKA ACT IN 1854, WHICH ALLOWED THOSE TWO TERRITORIES TO DETERMINE THE LEGALITY OF SLAVERY FOR THEMSELVES AND VIRTUALLY NULLIFIED THE MISSOURI COMPROMISE.

1854: CLEVELAND, OHIO

FIRST THE FUGITIVE SLAVE ACT, NOW THE KANSAS-NEBRASKA BILL.

WHAT'S NEXT, SLAVERY IN THE NORTH? I'VE SAID FOR YEARS THAT BLACK MEN AND WOMEN CONSTITUTE A "NATION WITHIN A NATION." OUR ONLY HOPE IS FOR OUR "NATION" TO LEAVE THE BORDERS OF THE UNITED STATES.

CLAP! CLAP! CLAP! CLAP! CLAP! CLAP! CLAP! CLAP!

MEN LIKE FREDERICK DOUGLASS SAY THAT WHAT BROTHER DELANY AND I PROPOSE IS DESTRUCTIVE TO OUR PEOPLE'S BEST INTEREST.

WELL, I SAY TO THEM THAT TO STAND STILL IS TO STAGNATE AND DIE.

FOR THAT REASON I AM WILLING TO SEEK ON OTHER SHORES THE FREEDOM WHICH HAS BEEN DENIED TO ME IN THE LAND OF MY BIRTH.

THERE WAS NO MASS EXODUS FROM THE UNITED STATES AFTER THE CONVENTION. BUT SOME OF THE ATTENDEES, INCLUDING MARTIN DELANY, MOVED TO THE GROWING BLACK SETTLEMENT OF CHATHAM, ONTARIO.

ALL ABOARD FOR CANADA!

THE KANSAS-NEBRASKA ACT SPURRED MANY SYMPATHETIC WHITE PEOPLE TO ACTION, AND IN 1854 THE REPUBLICAN PARTY WAS FOUNDED. ONE PLANK OF ITS PLATFORM WAS THE CONTAINMENT OF SLAVERY.

MEANWHILE, OTHER FREE BLACKS TOOK THE POSITION THAT KNOWLEDGE IS POWER.

THE MIRROR of the TIMES

ADVICE TO BLACK CALIFORNIANS

Chelsea Bank Might Pay All
Superintendent of Banks,

Negro Appointments
WASHINGTON, D.C.— The Senate Tuesday of last week confirmed the nomination of Charles E. Mitchell of Institute, W. Va., as United States minister resident and consul general to Liberia. He is

ab i Stands For Identity
Plans for Parallel Negro Institutions With Whites

IN 1855 IN CALIFORNIA, MIFFLIN GIBBS PUBLISHED THE STATE'S FIRST BLACK NEWSPAPER, THE MIRROR OF THE TIMES.

IN 1856, THE AFRICAN METHODIST EPISCOPAL CHURCH FOUNDED WILBERFORCE COLLEGE IN OHIO.

THAT SAME YEAR, A BLACK CALIFORNIA WOMAN NAMED BIDDY MASON WAS GRANTED HER FREEDOM BY THE STATE COURT.
THROUGHOUT HER LIFE SHE WOULD DONATE HER TIME AND MONEY TO SCHOOLS, CHURCHES, AND NURSING HOMES.
SHE WOULD BE REMEMBERED AS ONE OF CALIFORNIA'S FINEST HUMANITARIANS.

BUT SOON BLACK AMERICA WOULD BE HIT WITH A SUBSTANTIAL SETBACK.

DRED SCOTT AND HIS WIFE HELEN WERE SLAVES TRAVELING WITH THEIR OWNER, JOHN EMERSON, AN ARMY OFFICER WHO WAS FIRST STATIONED IN ILLINOIS, THEN IN THE WISCONSIN TERRITORY, AND FINALLY IN MISSOURI, WHERE HE DIED IN 1846.

NOW THAT HE'S DEAD, FREEDOM'S 'ROUND THE CORNER.

THE SCOTTS THEN SUED EMERSON'S WIDOW FOR THEIR FREEDOM IN THE MISSOURI COURTS.

IT IS QUITE ELEMENTARY. MY CLIENTS HAVE LIVED IN TWO PLACES WHERE SLAVERY HAS BEEN BANNED: ILLINOIS AND THE WISCONSIN TERRITORY. FOR THAT REASON THEY MUST BE CONSIDERED FREE CITIZENS OF THE GREAT STATE OF MISSOURI.

1852:

THE COURT RULES AGAINST THE SCOTTS, AND HEREBY DECLARES THAT THEY SHALL REMAIN SLAVES.

THE SCOTTS TOOK THE CASE TO THE U.S. SUPREME COURT.

BOTH OF YOU ARE WRONG! FIRSTLY, NEGROES ARE AN INFERIOR SPECIES, AND HAVE NO RIGHTS A WHITE MAN NEEDS TO RESPECT.
SECONDLY, **NEITHER** FREE **NEGROES NOR SLAVES ARE CITIZENS,** THEREFORE THEY HAVE NO RIGHT TO USE THE FEDERAL COURTS. AND FINALLY, DEPRIVING AN INDIVIDUAL OF PROPERTY SOLELY BECAUSE THE OWNER HAS TAKEN THAT PROPERTY INTO A DIFFERENT TERRITORY IS A VIOLATION OF THE CONSTITUTION.

THE SCOTTS SHOULD BE FREED. THE MISSOURI COMPROMISE CLEARLY SUPPORTS THEIR POSITION.

PRECISELY.

DESPITE THE DISSENTING OPINIONS OF JOHN MCLEAN AND BENJAMIN CURTIS, CHIEF JUSTICE ROGER TANEY'S POSITION PREVAILED, AND NOT ONLY DID THE SCOTTS REMAIN SLAVES, BUT ALL BLACKS WERE DENIED CITIZENSHIP BECAUSE OF THEIR RACE...

... AND THE LIVES OF FREE BLACKS GREW MORE TENUOUS.

IN 1858, MARYLAND BANNED BLACK PEOPLE FROM OPERATING BOATS ON THE POTOMAC RIVER.

IN ARKANSAS, FREE BLACKS WERE GIVEN AN ULTIMATUM BY THE STATE LEGISLATURE.

IF THE FREE NIGGERS WANT TO STAY FREE, THEN THEY'D BETTER LEAVE THE STATE OF ARKANSAS.

BROWN HAD HOPED TO GET THE EAR OF MARTIN DELANY IN CHATHAM.

IN RESPONSE, ON MAY 8, 1858, AN ANTI SLAVERY CONVENTION WAS SPONSORED IN CHATHAM, ONTARIO, BY A WHITE MAN NAMED JOHN BROWN.

103

I PROPOSE AN INDEPENDENT COMMUNITY TO BE ESTABLISHED WITHIN THE UNITED STATES, BUT WITHOUT STATE SOVEREIGNTY.

I'M OSBORNE ANDERSON. I'LL JOIN UP WITH YOU.

GOOD LUCK, BUT MY PEOPLE'S FUTURE LIES OUTSIDE OF AMERICAN BORDERS.

SO WITH ONE NEW RECRUIT JOHN BROWN CONTINUED WITH HIS PLAN.

MEANWHILE, BACK IN THE UNITED STATES...

SINCE THE DAYS OF PAUL CUFFE AND JAMES FORTEN, BLACKS WERE SUCCESSFUL IN MARITIME INDUSTRIES. THAT TREND CONTINUED IN NEW ENGLAND, WHERE BLACKS WERE VIEWED FAVORABLY WITHIN THE WHALING INDUSTRY. IN FACT, A BLACK MAN NAMED LEWIS TEMPLE HAD REVOLUTIONIZED WHALING BY INVENTING THE TOGGLE HARPOON IN 1848. BY THE 1850s, WHALING WAS ONE OF THE FEW INDUSTRIES IN THE U.S. ECONOMY WHERE BLACK AND WHITE MEN WORKED UNDER ANYTHING CLOSE TO EQUAL CONDITIONS.

IN BALTIMORE, BLACK PEOPLE DOMINATED THE CATERING INDUSTRY TO SUCH A DEGREE THAT MANY WHITES IN MARYLAND WANTED TO MAKE BLACK BUSINESS PARTICIPATION ILLEGAL, BUT DECIDED AGAINST IT BECAUSE THE MARYLAND ECONOMY DEPENDED ON THE LABOR OF FREE BLACKS.

NONETHELESS, THE STRIVINGS OF A FEW COULDN'T PREVENT TWO EVENTS THAT WOULD LEAD TO THE TRANSFORMATION OF AMERICAN SOCIETY.

ON OCTOBER 16, 1859, IN HARPERS FERRY, VIRGINIA, JOHN BROWN PUT HIS PLAN FOR AN INDEPENDENT COMMUNITY INTO ACTION.

HE AND HIS MEN SEIZED A MUNITIONS STOREHOUSE IN ORDER TO OVERTHROW SLAVERY AND BUILD A NEW COMMUNITY.

UNFORTUNATELY, THE CONDUCTOR OF A PASSING TRAIN TOLD THE AUTHORITIES WHAT HE HAD SEEN.

BROWN'S MEN FOUND THEMSELVES BATTLING MILITARY FORCES BEFORE LONG.

BROWN AND SOME OF HIS MEN WERE CAPTURED AND EXECUTED, BUT OSBORNE ANDERSON, BROWN'S RECRUIT FROM CHATHAM, ESCAPED.

DESPITE THE EXECUTIONS, BLACKS AND MASSES OF NORTHERN WHITES SAW JOHN BROWN AS A HERO AND A MARTYR. THAT OFFENDED THE PRO-SLAVERY SOUTHERNERS, AND PUSHED THE UNION ONE STEP CLOSER TO CRISIS."

THE STRAW THAT BROKE THE CAMEL'S BACK WAS THE ELECTION OF ABRAHAM LINCOLN TO THE PRESIDENCY. LINCOLN'S REPUBLICAN PLATFORM OPPOSED THE EXPANSION OF SLAVERY, AND WAS PERCEIVED AS ABOLITIONIST BY MANY SOUTHERNERS.

NOW THAT THAT DANGED LINCOLN'S IN OFFICE IT WON'T BE LONG BEFORE THEM YANKEES TAKE AWAY OUR STATES' RIGHTS AND TRY TO KEEP US FROM TAKING OUR SLAVES WHERE WE WANT. BEFORE LONG THEY'LL ABOLISH SLAVERY.

YEAH, IT'S HIGH TIME WE TAKE A STAND.

BY LATE 1860, SOUTH CAROLINA AND SIX OTHER STATES HAD SECEDED FROM THE UNION, PROTESTING LINCOLN'S ELECTION. AND IN FEBRUARY 1861, JEFFERSON DAVIS, A U.S. SENATOR FROM MISSISSIPPI, WAS ELECTED PRESIDENT OF THE NEWLY FORMED CONFEDERACY.

ON APRIL 12, 1861, CONFEDERATE CANNONS BEGAN SHELLING UNION FORCES HOLED UP AT FORT SUMTER IN CHARLESTON, SOUTH CAROLINA, AND AMERICA'S CIVIL WAR WAS LAUNCHED.

THE CONFEDERACY GOT THE UPPER HAND AT THE OUTSET OF THE WAR.

UNDETERRED, SLAVES CONTINUED TO RISK THEIR LIVES FOR FREEDOM. MARY PEAKE, A FREE BLACK WOMAN, ESTABLISHED A SCHOOL FOR RUNAWAY SLAVES AT FORTRESS MONROE, VIRGINIA, WITH THE HELP OF WHITE PHILANTHROPIST LEWIS TAPPAN.

AS THE WAR PROGRESSED, THOUSANDS OF SLAVES POURED OVER UNION LINES IN SEARCH OF SANCTUARY. THEY BECAME KNOWN AS "CONTRABAND."

UNDER THE FUGITIVE SLAVE ACT, RUNAWAY SLAVES HAD TO BE RETURNED TO THEIR MASTERS. THEY COULDN'T BE FREED. PROCLAIMING THEM CONTRABAND OF WAR MEANT THAT THE UNITED STATES GOVERNMENT OWNED THOUSANDS OF PEOPLE WITHIN UNION LINES. WHAT WAS TO BE DONE WITH THEM?

IN AUGUST OF 1862, PRESIDENT LINCOLN CALLED TOGETHER A GROUP OF INFLUENTIAL BLACK PEOPLE TO DISCUSS THE REMOVAL OF THE BLACK POPULATION FROM THE UNITED STATES, BOTH FREE AND CONTRABAND.

YOUR RACE SUFFER GREATLY BY LIVING AMONG US, WHILE OURS SUFFER FROM YOUR PRESENCE. IN A WORD, WE SUFFER ON EACH SIDE. IF THIS IS ADMITTED IT AFFORDS A REASON WHY WE SHOULD BE SEPARATED.

EXCUSE US, MR. PRESIDENT, WE MUST TALK THIS OVER.

PERHAPS THE PRESIDENT IS RIGHT. PERHAPS IT WOULD BE BETTER FOR BOTH RACES IF WE LEAVE.

NONSENSE. BLACK MEN AND WOMEN ARE STRUGGLING FOR THEIR FREEDOM. WE CANNOT ABANDON THEM IN THEIR TIME OF NEED.

ROBERT SMALLS, A SHIP PILOT, WAS FORCED BY CONFEDERATE SOLDIERS TO AID THE CONFEDERATE ARMY.

SCRUB THE DECK, BOY.

ON MAY 13, 1862, SMALLS TOOK THE HELM OF A CONFEDERATE GUNBOAT NAMED THE PLANTER.
A SKILLED SAILOR, HE SIMPLY TURNED THE BOAT AROUND AND GAVE IT OVER TO THE UNION ARMY.

BUT SUCH SYMBOLISM ALONE COULD NOT WIN WARS. SOME WHITE NORTHERNERS WERE LESS THAN ENTHUSIASTIC ABOUT BLACK RIGHTS.
THEY WERE KNOWN AS "COPPERHEADS."

THE HEROICS OF PEOPLE LIKE ROBERT SMALLS AS WELL AS THE PRESSURES OF INTERNATIONAL POLITICS FORCED PRESIDENT LINCOLN TO RE-EVALUATE HIS THOUGHTS ON BLACK DEPORTATION.
ON JANUARY 1, 1863, HE ISSUED THE **EMANCIPATION PROCLAMATION**, FREEING THE SLAVES IN THE CONFEDERATE TERRITORIES AND TURNING THE WAR INTO A WAR OVER SLAVERY.
THIS PREVENTED THE UNITED KINGDOM AND FRANCE FROM RECOGNIZING THE CONFEDERACY AND SELLING IT GOODS AND WAR MATERIEL.

THE ONLY WAY WE CAN GET OUTTA FIGHTIN' TO FREE A BUNCHA NIGGERS IS IF WE PAY THE GOVERNMENT A 300 DOLLAR WAIVER. WHO THE HELL HAS 300 DOLLARS? I TELL YA, THE RICH FOLKS GET ALL THE BREAKS, THE NIGGERS GET ALL THE SYMPATHY, AND WORKIN' PEOPLE LIKE US GET ALL THE HARD TIMES.

YOU CAN SAY THAT AGAIN. I BET AS SOON AS WE GO AWAY TO FIGHT, NIGGERS LIKE THAT ONE OVER THERE'LL STEAL OUR JOBS.

IF YOU ASK ME, IF THERE WEREN'T NO NIGGERS WE WOULDN'T HAVE THIS PROBLEM. FAR AS I'M CONCERNED IT'S THE NIGGERS WE SHOULD BE FIGHTIN' IN THE FIRST PLACE.

YOU'RE DAMN RIGHT!

DON'T FIGHT FOR THE NIGGERS. FIGHT THE NIGGERS!

CRASH!

THE DRAFT RIOTS IN NEW YORK CITY IN 1863 LASTED 4 DAYS, AS WHITE IRISHMEN TERRORIZED THE STREETS, SET FIRE TO BLACK INSTITUTIONS, KILLED AT LEAST 11 BLACK PEOPLE AND MAIMED COUNTLESS OTHERS. WITH A BODY COUNT TOTALING AT LEAST 105, THE RIOT IS REMEMBERED AS THE MOST VIOLENT ONE IN AMERICAN HISTORY.

THAT SAME YEAR, THE BLACK COMMITTEE WAS FORMED BY THE UNITED STATES GOVERNMENT TO RECRUIT FREE BLACKS FOR THE UNION ARMY. MANY MEMBERS OF THE COMMITTEE WERE EMIGRATIONISTS, LIKE MARTIN DELANY, WHILE OTHERS WERE BELIEVERS IN THE AMERICAN WAY OF LIFE, LIKE FREDERICK DOUGLASS. THEY PUT ASIDE THEIR DIFFERENT IDEOLOGIES TO STRIKE A BLOW AGAINST A COMMON ENEMY, AMERICAN RACISM.

WE MUST ANSWER THE CALL. OUR GOVERNMENT NEEDS US.

NOT OUR GOVERNMENT, OUR PEOPLE.

AS A RESULT OF THE BLACK COMMITTEE'S EFFORTS, MANY BRAVE BLACK UNION REGIMENTS WERE FORMED. REGIMENTS LIKE THE FIFTY-FOURTH VOLUNTEER REGIMENT OF MASSACHUSETTS, THE EIGHTH U.S. COLORED OF PENNSYLVANIA, AND THE FIRST NORTH CAROLINA COLORED ALL FOUGHT WITH DISTINCTION.

AS THE UNION ARMY'S FORCES GREW AND OVERWHELMED THE CONFEDERACY, GENERAL ROBERT E. LEE SURRENDERED TO GENERAL ULYSSES S. GRANT ON APRIL 9, 1865.

DON'T BELIEVE FOR A MINUTE THAT THE WAR DID SLAVERY IN. IT WAS 246 YEARS OF OUR CREATIVITY AND STRUGGLE THAT PUT AN END TO SLAVERY.

WITH A LITTLE HELP FROM THE UNION ARMY.

WHAT SHOULD WE DO ABOUT THE SOUTH?

WITH THE WAR OVER, THE QUESTION OF HOW TO TREAT THE SOUTH AROSE.
SHOULD IT BE TREATED AS A CONQUERED NATION?
OR LIKE AN OLD FRIEND WITH WHOM THE NORTH HAD HAD A BRIEF ARGUMENT? AND WHAT OF BLACK FOLKS — SHOULD THEY BE AIDED AFTER 246 YEARS OF SUBJUGATION, OR SHOULD THEY BE LEFT TO FEND FOR THEMSELVES?
THE FEDERAL GOVERNMENT'S ATTEMPT TO ANSWER THESE QUESTIONS CAME TO BE KNOWN AS RECONSTRUCTION.

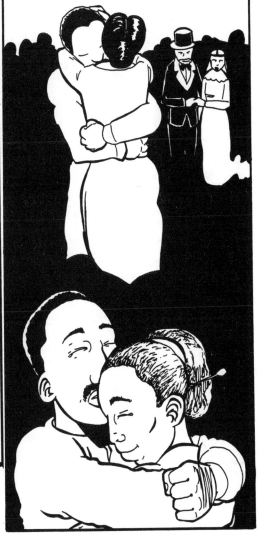

AT FIRST, BLACK WOMEN AND MEN WERE JUBILANT OVER THEIR FREEDOM. THROUGHOUT THE SOUTH, THE NEWLY FREED PEOPLE TRIED TO REBUILD FAMILIES THAT HAD BEEN SOLD APART. THEY TRAVELED MILES TO FIND ONE ANOTHER, AND IN MANY CASES, MASS WEDDINGS WERE HELD TO FORMALIZE BONDS THAT HAD BEEN BROKEN IN THE BLEAK DAYS OF SLAVERY.

MEANWHILE, SLAVEOWNERS WERE CONFUSED BY THE DESERTION OF SLAVES THEY THOUGHT WERE HAPPY AND LOYAL SERVANTS.

I TREATED THOSE NIGGERS LIKE FAMILY.

AS TIME PASSED, A FEW BLACK MEN AND WOMEN TRIED TO MAKE THE MOST OF THEIR FREE STATUS. IN SOUTH CAROLINA, GENERAL WILLIAM SHERMAN'S SPECIAL FIELD ORDER 15 ENABLED THEM TO WORK AND LIVE ON LAND CONFISCATED BY THE UNION ARMY.

I HAVE GOOD REASON TO BELIEVE THAT PRESIDENT LINCOLN WILL MAKE THIS LAND OFFICIALLY YOURS.

FOR THE VAST MAJORITY WHO WERE LANDLESS AND HOMELESS, A GOVERNMENT AGENCY— THE BUREAU OF REFUGEES, FREEDMEN, AND ABANDONED LAND, ALSO KNOWN AS THE FREEDMEN'S BUREAU — PROVIDED FOOD AND CLOTHING.

THE BUREAU WAS ALSO SUPPOSED TO DIVIDE THE CONQUERED AND ABANDONED SOUTHERN LAND INTO FORTY-ACRE PLOTS TO BE RENTED OR SOLD TO FREED BLACKS AND SYMPATHETIC WHITES.

THE UNION ARMY WOULD GIVE THE NEW LANDOWNERS MULES.

SURE, AND SANTA CLAUS WOULD GIVE THEM HORSES AND PLOWS.

APRIL 14, 1865: PRESIDENT LINCOLN'S CABINET MEETING.

BUT FOR LINCOLN, FORTY ACRES AND A MULE WAS NOT THE POLITICALLY SOUND THING TO DO.

I WANT NO PERSECUTION...

ALL WE NEED TO DO IS ENFORCE THE BASIC CONSTITUTIONAL AND LEGAL RIGHTS OF THE FREEDMEN.

THERE IS NO NEED TO DRAMATICALLY RESTRUCTURE THE SOUTH WITH ANY TYPE OF LAND REFORM.

THAT NIGHT, ABRAHAM LINCOLN WAS SHOT BY A CRAZED CONFEDERATE ZEALOT. HE DIED THE NEXT DAY.

WITH LINCOLN DEAD, ANDREW JOHNSON BECAME PRESIDENT. JOHNSON GAVE THE IMPRESSION THAT HE WOULD BE MORE COMMITTED THAN LINCOLN TO RECONSTRUCTION.

THE ACT OF TREASON OF THE CONFEDERATES MUST BE MADE INFAMOUS, AND THOSE REBEL TRAITORS MUST BE PUNISHED. WE MUST RECONSTRUCT THE SOUTH.

NOTHIN' BUT A PACK OF LIES.

... INSTEAD OF PUNISHMENT, HE GAVE WHOLESALE PARDONS TO PROMINENT AND RICH FORMER CONFEDERATES.

THESE PARDONS HAD A PERMANENT EFFECT ON AMERICA.

THE PARDONED WERE ALLOWED TO RECLAIM LAND THAT FREED MEN AND WOMEN HAD SETTLED ON AND COUNTED ON TO BUILD NEW LIVES. NO ONE COULD SAY THEY HADN'T WORKED FOR IT OR FOUGHT FOR IT.

NEXT HE ATTEMPTED TO VETO THE CIVIL RIGHTS ACT OF 1865 GUARANTEEING BLACK PEOPLE ACCESS TO PUBLIC ACCOMMODATIONS.

HE FAILED, BUT HIS EFFORTS WERE A CALL TO ARMS FOR RACIST SOUTHERNERS.

THIS IS OUR LAND, BOY. HOPE YA DIDN'T GET TOO COMFORTABLE WITH IT.

UNDER JOHNSON'S ADMINISTRATION, WHITE TERRORIST ORGANIZATIONS LIKE THE KU KLUX KLAN AND THE KNIGHTS OF THE WHITE CAMELLIA FORMED WITHOUT ANY INTERFERENCE FROM THE LAW OR OBJECTION FROM THOSE IN POWER.

IN CONGRESS, NORTHERN REPUBLICANS GREW DISGRUNTLED WITH JOHNSON.

IF WE LET JOHNSON FLY IN THE FACE OF OUR RECONSTRUCTION EFFORTS THEN THE REPUBLICAN PARTY IS DOOMED.

THAT IDIOT JOHNSON IS GIVING THE REBEL SOUTHERNERS TOO MUCH POWER.

PERHAPS, BUT SURELY WE CANNOT EXPECT SUPPORT FROM THE SOUTHERNERS. THEY HATE REPUBLICANS.

THE **WHITE** ONES HATE US. THE BLACK ONES LOVE US. THEY ARE THE ONES WHOSE POLITICAL EFFORTS WE SHOULD SUPPORT.

WE'D BE DOING THE BLACKS A BETTER SERVICE IF WE GAVE THEM LAND, AND NOT JUST THE RIGHT TO VOTE.

COME NOW, THADDEUS. LET US NOT GET CARRIED AWAY.

IN 1867, THE REPUBLICAN-CONTROLLED CONGRESS PASSED THE RECONSTRUCTION ACT, DIVIDING THE SOUTH INTO FEDERALLY OCCUPIED TERRITORIES.

IN SOME OF THOSE TERRITORIES, BLACKS HAD A MAJORITY, AND WERE ELECTED TO STATE OFFICES.

SOUTHERN LAND

WITH THE BACKING OF THE RADICAL REPUBLICANS IN CONGRESS, BLACK MALE SOUTHERNERS ORGANIZED POLITICAL CLUBS KNOWN AS UNION LEAGUES. THE UNION LEAGUES PROVIDED THEM WITH SOME POLITICAL CLOUT.

I'VE WAITED MY WHOLE LIFE TO VOTE.

Scrach! scrich!

1 2 3 4 5 6 7 8 9 10 11 12 13 14 15 16 17 18 19...

REPUBLICAN PARTY

BUT THE BIG WINNERS IN THE LATE 1860s AND EARLY 1870s WERE THE WHITE REPUBLICANS THEMSELVES.

WITH THE HELP OF BLACK UNION LEAGUE ORGANIZERS, THE REPUBLICANS GAINED CONTROL OF THE STATE GOVERNMENTS IN THE SOUTH.

VOTE REPUBLICAN

THE REPUBLICANS AND THE UNION LEAGUE'LL GUARD COLORED FOLKS' RIGHTS.

VOTE REPUBLIC

FOR THE MOST PART, BLACK REPUBLICAN POLITICIANS WORKED IN THE SHADOW OF THEIR WHITE COUNTERPARTS, BUT WHEREVER POSSIBLE THEY LEFT THEIR MARK. IN SOUTH CAROLINA, FOR A BRIEF TIME, BLACKS MADE UP MORE THAN 65 PERCENT OF THE LOWER HOUSE OF THE STATE LEGISLATURE AND WORKED HARD TO REFORM THE STATE'S DEMOCRATIC SYSTEM.

SOUTH CAROLINA STATE LEGISLATURE

THEY ENACTED LAWS TO MAKE COMMON SCHOOLS AVAILABLE TO MOST CHILDREN,, BLACK AS WELL AS WHITE.

THE BLACK MAJORITY LEGISLATURE ALSO ELIMINATED DEBTORS' PRISONS AND ABOLISHED THE WHIPPING OF PRISONERS.

AS LONG AS I AM IN OFFICE, I WILL NOT LET A MAN FEEL THE WHIP, NO MATTER WHAT THE CRIME.

BUT POLITICAL CLOUT WENT ONLY SO FAR, AND ON THE ECONOMIC FRONT, THE FORMER SLAVES DIDN'T FARE SO WELL.

TELL THE TRUTH, NOW: WE HAD IT JUST AS BAD AS WE DID BACK IN SLAVERY.

HAD WE GOT OUR FORTY ACRES AND A MULE, LOTS OF US WOULD HAVE BEEN LANDOWNING FARMERS. INSTEAD WE BECAME LANDLESS SHARECROPPERS. IN THIS SYSTEM, THE FORMER SLAVES SOLD THEIR LABOR FOR A SHARE OF THE CROPS. ALL SUPPLIES NEEDED TO FARM WERE BOUGHT FROM THE LANDOWNER ON CREDIT AND PAID OFF WITH THE PROFITS FROM THE LABORERS' SHARE OF THE CROPS. THOSE PRICES WERE NOT FIXED. IN FACT, THE FARMERS CHARGED ANY PRICE THEY WANTED,

AND THE SHARECROPPERS EASILY BECAME TRAPPED IN DEBT.

IT WAS A HARD, HARD LIFE.

I COULDA SWORE THEY TOLE ME LINCOLN FREED US.

BUT IT WASN'T SLAVERY, AND MANY WHITES FELT THAT THE FORMER SLAVES HAD RISEN TOO HIGH, TOO FAST.

THAT'LL TEACH THEM NIGGERS AND THEIR 'NIGGER-LOVIN' FRIENDS A LESSON.

SLOWLY THE ACTS OF TERRORISM BEGAN TO TAKE THEIR TOLL ON BLACK PEOPLE, AND WHITE DEMOCRATS BEGAN TO REGAIN CONTROL.

BALLOT BOX

AND IF THE VIOLENCE WEREN'T ENOUGH, MANY RADICAL REPUBLICANS' INTERESTS TURNED FROM JUSTICE FOR BLACK PEOPLE TO PROFITS FOR WHITE PEOPLE.

THIS FREEDMEN'S BUREAU IS A FINANCIAL DRAIN. BESIDES, NEGROES HAVE BEEN FREE FOR ALMOST THREE YEARS— HOW MUCH MORE HELP DO THEY NEED? THE MONEY COULD BE PUT TO BETTER USE BY EXPANDING THE RAILROADS.

PRECISELY.

IN 1872, THE FREEDMEN'S BUREAU WAS SHUT DOWN AND THE FEDERAL GOVERNMENT PAID LITTLE HEED TO BLACK SOUTHERNERS' NEED FOR PROTECTION FROM VIOLENT WHITE SUPREMACISTS.

FREEDMEN'S BUREAU

"OUT OF" BUSINESS

CLOP. CLOP. CLOP!

AS ALWAYS, THOUGH, THERE WERE INDIVIDUAL TRIUMPHS. IN 1872, ELIJAH McCOY EARNED A PATENT FOR A STEAM ENGINE LUBRICATOR. THIS WAS THE FIRST OF McCOY'S MANY INVENTIONS.
IN YEARS TO COME McCOY'S WORK WOULD BE SO PRODIGIOUS THAT THE PHRASE **THE REAL McCOY** WOULD BE COINED IN HIS HONOR.

THAT'S RIGHT.

BUT NOT EVEN THE REAL McCOY COULD INVENT A GADGET TO END RACISM AND DECEPTION. IN 1876, THE PRESIDENTIAL ELECTION BETWEEN REPUBLICAN RUTHERFORD B. HAYES AND DEMOCRAT SAMUEL J. TILDEN HAD RESULTED IN TILDEN WINNING THE POPULAR VOTE, BUT SECRETLY A DEAL WAS ABOUT TO BE MADE...

AS YOU KNOW WE'RE ALREADY DISPUTING 20 OF TILDEN'S ELECTORAL VOTES, 19 OF WHICH COME FROM THE SOUTH. NOW IF YOU DEMOCRATS CAST YOUR ELECTORAL VOTES FOR HAYES WITHOUT A FUSS, THEN WE PROMISE YOU GENTS THAT WE'LL STAY OUT OF YOUR BUSINESS IN THE SOUTH.

YOU'VE GOT YO' SELF A DEAL.

IN 1876, RUTHERFORD B. HAYES BECAME PRESIDENT IN A SUSPICIOUS ELECTION, AND THE ERA OF RECONSTRUCTION ENDED.

WITH RECONSTRUCTION OVER, WHITE TERRORISM CONTINUED TO ESCALATE. IT GREW EXTREMELY DIFFICULT FOR BLACK WOMEN AND MEN TO LIVE IN PEACE.

IN 1877, SEVEN LAND DEVELOPERS— SIX BLACK, ONE WHITE — CAME UP WITH AN IDEA TO EASE THE BURDEN OF RECONSTRUCTION LIFE.

WHAT BLACK FOLKS NEED IS TO LIVE AWAY FROM WHITE FOLKS.

YES, AND WE CAN PROFIT FROM THIS NEED.

THEY FOUNDED THE ALL-BLACK TOWN OF NICODEMUS, KANSAS.

TWO YEARS LATER, PAP SINGLETON, A FORMER ESCAPED SLAVE, TOOK THE NICODEMUS IDEA A STEP FURTHER.

FREE KANSAS

SINGLETON CANVASSED THE SOUTH, BILLING THE ENTIRE STATE OF KANSAS AS A HAVEN FOR FORMER SLAVES. SOON MANY BLACKS FROM TEXAS, MISSISSIPPI, TENNESSEE, AND LOUISIANA WERE DOING ANYTHING THEY COULD TO GET TO KANSAS.

FREEDOM! AND PROSPERITY IN KANSAS

GO TO THE WIDE OPEN SPACES OF KANSAS. IT'S A PARADISE FOR COLORED FOLKS.

THEY DILIGENTLY SAVED MONEY FROM MENIAL JOBS TO GET TO KANSAS.

SAY BOY, IF YOU BURY MY HORSE I'LL PAY YOU TWO BITS.

HERE'S A NICKEL FOR YOUR HARD WORK, SADIE. I'LL SEE YOU TOMORROW.

NOT IF I CAN HELP IT.

FORMER SLAVES FLOCKED TO THE MIDWEST IN SEARCH OF **FREE KANSAS.** THEY WERE CALLED "EXODUSTERS."

THE WHITE PLANTERS' REACTION TO THE EXODUSTERS WAS ALL BUT ENTHUSIASTIC.

IF WE KEEP LETTIN' THEM NIGGERS GIT TA KANSAS, THEN WHO'S GONNA BRING IN THE HARVEST?

IT'S TIME WE PUT A END TA THIS WHOLE EXODUSTIN' FOOLISHNESS.

TO PROTECT THEIR ECONOMIC INTERESTS, A GROUP OF WHITES UNSUCCESSFULLY TRIED TO PERSUADE MISSISSIPPI RIVERBOAT OPERATORS NOT TO TAKE EXODUSTERS, AND SENT AGENTS TO ST. LOUIS TO TRY TO RETURN THE EXODUSTERS TO THE SOUTH.

FEARING THE SOUTH WOULD FIND SOME WAY TO PUT THEM BACK INTO SLAVERY, THE EXODUSTERS KEPT ON DESPITE THE OBSTACLES AND THE HARDSHIPS THAT AWAITED THEM IN KANSAS. MOST SETTLED IN TOWNS LIKE KANSAS CITY AND TOPEKA, WHERE THEY FOUND WORK.

WELCOME TO KANSAS

MEANWHILE, BACK IN THE SOUTHERN STATES, MILLIONS OF BLACK SHARECROPPERS WERE CONSTANTLY IN DEBT AND LIVING IN ABJECT POVERTY.

BUT THE 1880s AND EARLY 1890s ALSO SAW BLACKS ACHIEVE MORE IN SCIENCE AND TECHNOLOGY. IN 1882, LEWIS H. LATIMER, WHILE WORKING FOR HIRAM MAXIM'S UNITED STATES ELECTRIC LIGHTING COMPANY, PATENTED A PROCESS TO PRODUCE CARBON LIGHT-BULB FILAMENTS. HIS INVENTION WAS INSTRUMENTAL IN BRINGING LIGHT TO THE WORLD.

GRANVILLE T. WOODS WAS A GREAT INVENTOR IN THE RAILWAY INDUSTRY.

ONE OF HIS MOST FAMOUS INVENTIONS WAS THE "THIRD RAIL," WHICH GAVE POWER TO SUBWAY TRAINS.

AND JUST LIKE THEIR FORERUNNERS THE WORKSHOP SLAVES, THESE MEN WERE ABLE TO LIVE IN RELATIVE COMFORT BY IMPROVING THE WAY AMERICANS DID THINGS.

AHHH

DON'T BEAT ROUND THE BUSH, HERE'S THE WHOLE TRUTH, WHEN SLAVERY ENDED THERE WERE 120,000 SKILLED ARTISANS IN THE SOUTH; 100,000 OF THEM WERE BLACK. WHITE FOLKS STARTED TO TURN THAT AROUND LICKETY SPLIT. IN 1880 IN PLACES LIKE NASHVILLE, TENNESSEE, WHITE FOLKS LEARNED THEIR SKILLS FROM US.

AND THIS IS HOW YOU MAKE A BEVEL CUT, JAKE.

THEN THE FIRST CHANCE THEY GOT, THEY LOCKED US OUT OF THE SAME JOBS WE TRAINED THEM FOR.

CARPENTERS WANTED

NIGRAS NEED NOT APPLY.

SO THOUGH TECHNOLOGY HELPED A VERY, VERY, VERY SMALL NUMBER OF US SUCCEED, TRICK-KNOWLEDGE-Y WAS DOING US IN. AND IN ORDER TO WITHSTAND TRICK-KNOWLEDGE-Y, ONE MAN TURNED TO THEOLOGY. AS A BISHOP IN THE AME CHURCH, HENRY McNEAL TURNER COMBINED THE EMIGRATION ASPIRATIONS OF PAUL CUFFE WITH THE "NATION WITHIN A NATION" PHILOSOPHY OF MARTIN DELANY, BUT ADDED A POWERFUL RELIGIOUS SPIRIT.

GOD IS A NEGRO!

THAT WAS A POWERFUL SERMON, BISHOP TURNER.

BY GIVING BLACK PEOPLE A STRONGER SENSE OF CLOSENESS TO DIVINITY AND BY PAINTING AFRICA AS A HOMELAND FOR THE EMBATTLED FORMER SLAVE POPULATION, TURNER ATTRACTED A MASS FOLLOWING IN GEORGIA.

BUT IN THIS LAND, THERE WAS STILL A ROUGH REALITY FOR BLACK PEOPLE TO DEAL WITH.

COME ON, BOY, WE'RE ARRESTIN' YA FOR STEALIN' OLD MAN CUMBERBATCH'S HOG.

YOIKS!

UNDER THE CONVICT-LEASING PROGRAM STARTED IN THE MID-1880s, MANY BLACK PEOPLE WERE THROWN IN JAIL ON TRUMPED-UP CHARGES AND THEN HIRED OUT TO WORK FOR WHITE MEN BY THE PRISONS THAT INCARCERATED THEM. THE SYSTEM WORKED TO THE ADVANTAGE OF THE PRISONS.

THAT'S AN UNDERSTATEMENT. THE PRISONS, THE EMPLOYERS, AND THE STATE MADE OUT LIKE BANDITS. THEY DIDN'T GIVE A DAMN ABOUT THE BLACK MEN THEY FORCED TO WORK FOR NOTHING.

THE MONEY WAS PURE PROFIT FOR THE PRISONS AND THE STATES, WHILE THE EMPLOYER GOT HIMSELF THE PERFECT LOW-WAGE SYSTEM OF FORCED LABOR.

WHITE FOLKS GOT ALL THE MONEY, ALL THE LAND AND ALL THE CREDIT. ALL WE GOT IS DEBT. I DON'T SEE HOW WE GONNA MAKE IT.

WE JUST GONNA HAVE TO GO ALONG TO GET ALONG.

IT WAS DURING THIS RISING TIDE OF RACISM THAT BLACK SURVIVAL STRATEGIES TOOK AN AMBITIOUS, BUT DESPERATE, TURN.

ONE EXAMPLE WAS THE TOWN OF MOUND BAYOU, MISSISSIPPI. FOUNDED IN 1887, MOUND BAYOU WAS THE BRAINCHILD OF AN INFLUENTIAL, ENTERPRISING FORMER MISSISSIPPI WORKSHOP SLAVE NAMED ISAIAH MONTGOMERY.

NEGROES IN MISSISSIPPI COULD LIVE WELL IF THEY HAD THEIR OWN TOWN.

HOW THEY GONNA DO THAT?

WHATEVER IT TAKES, IT WILL BE DONE.

TRUE TO HIS WORD, MONTGOMERY MADE SURE THAT MOUND BAYOU HAD THE RESOURCES TO MEET THE NEEDS OF ITS INHABITANTS, AND FOR A TIME IT WAS A HAVEN FOR BLACK FOLKS IN MISSISSIPPI. BUT ITS STATUS CAME AT A HIGH PRICE.

AT THE SAME TIME, AMERICA WAS MOVING INTO THE MACHINE AGE. FARMS WERE BEING REPLACED BY FACTORIES, RAILROADS AND TELEGRAPHS SPED UP THE PACE OF LIFE, AND MONOPOLIES AND TRUSTS PUT THE SQUEEZE ON SMALL BUSINESSES, FARMERS AND LABORERS. MANY AMERICANS GREW SUSPICIOUS OF INDUSTRY.

THIS COUNTRY IS GETTIN' WORSE BY THE DAY. THEM DAMN PLUTOCRATS ARE TRYIN' TA TAKE ALL THE MONEY.

AMEN TO THAT. IT'S GETTIN' SO BAD THAT A FELLA CAIN'T MAKE AN HONEST BUCK. I TELL YA, I'M FIXIN' FOR A CHANGE.

THAT CHANGE THE FARMERS WERE "FIXIN' FOR" BECAME THE POPULIST MOVEMENT OF THE 1890s.

FROM THE BEGINNING, BLACK FARMERS WERE AN INTEGRAL PART OF THE POPULIST MOVEMENT.

YA' KNOW SOMETHIN' FREEMAN, THEM WHITE POPULISTS JEST MIGHT BE ON TA SOMETHIN'.

YEAH, MAYBE IF WE JOIN UP WITH EM' WE'LL GET SOME PROTECTION WHEN WE TRY TO VOTE.

YOU BOYS SOUND SERIOUS ABOUT POPULISM.

INDEED WE ARE. WE'RE FARMERS — HOW CAN WE JOIN THAT THERE FARMERS' ALLIANCE?

YOU CAN'T EXACTLY JOIN IT. YA SEE, IT'S FOR WHITE MEN ONLY.

AW HELL, HERE WE GO AGAIN. WE MIGHT AS WELL HEAD ON BACK HOME, JEFFERSON.

YOUR FRIEND DIDN'T LET ME FINISH. JEST CAUSE YOU CAN'T JOIN THE FARMERS' ALLIANCE DON'T MEAN YOU CAN'T BE A POPULIST. HELL, YOU CAN START YOUR OWN COLORED FARMERS' ALLIANCE, AND JOIN THE POPULISTS THAT WAY.

SOON THERE WAS A COLORED FARMERS' ALLIANCE. BUT IT FELL APART OVER A FAILED COTTON-PICKING STRIKE IN 1889.

NONETHELESS, BLACK PEOPLE HAD CLOUT WITH THE POPULISTS — ESPECIALLY IN NORTH CAROLINA.

IN 1894, A COALITION OF BLACK REPUBLICANS AND WHITE POPULISTS GAINED CONTROL OF THE NORTH CAROLINA LEGISLATURE.

SOON BLACK OFFICE-HOLDING BECAME COMMON IN THE EASTERN BLACK BELT OF THE STATE.

NORTH CAROLINA LEGISLATURE

REPUBLICAN

POPULIST

SOUTHERN DEMOCRAT

BLACK-WHITE ALLIANCES LIKE THOSE HORRIFIED THE EXISTING POWER STRUCTURE.

WE MUST DO SOMETHING ABOUT THE POPULISTS.

125

BUT COALITION POLITICS IS TRICKY AND THE OPPONENTS OF POPULISM WERE RESOURCEFUL. SOON THEY WERE ABLE TO EXPLOIT THE RACISM INHERENT IN AMERICAN, AND ESPECIALLY SOUTHERN, SOCIETY.

YOU FELLOWS KEEP WORKING WITH THE COLORED PEOPLE IF YOU WANT. BUT WHEN YOUR WIVES' HONOR IS TAKEN BY THOSE BEASTS, AND THEY BEAR LITTLE TAN MONGRELS, YOU'LL HAVE NOBODY TO BLAME BUT YOURSELVES.

IF YOU WORK WITH THE WHITE MAN IN THE DEMOCRATIC PARTY, AND FORGET THIS POPULIST NONSENSE, YOU WON'T HAVE TO WORRY ABOUT YOUR WIFE'S PURITY.

YOU KNOW, I THOUGHT I SAW ONE OF THOSE DARKIES GIVE MY LIZZIE THE EYE.

COULD BE.

YAAAH!

!RRiiiiP!

JUST

POPU

RACIST RUMORS RAVAGED THOSE POPULIST ALLIANCES, AND JUST AS IN RECONSTRUCTION, THE BIRTH OF A BLACK BODY POLITIC WAS ABORTED.

BUT IN THE MIDST OF ALL THE FALSE STARTS AND BETRAYALS ONE MAN FELT THAT HE HELD THE SOLUTION TO AMERICA'S RACIAL PROBLEM.

BOOKER T. WASHINGTON WAS SCHOOLED IN THE WORK ETHIC AND THE IMPORTANCE OF INDUSTRY AT THE HAMPTON INSTITUTE. THE LESSONS HE LEARNED AT HAMPTON INSPIRED HIM TO FOUND THE TUSKEGEE INSTITUTE IN ALABAMA IN 1881.

OVER TIME HE BUILT TUSKEGEE THROUGH HARD WORK...

... AND A DYNAMIC AND SHREWD PERSONALITY.

GENTLEMEN, IN YEARS TO COME MY INSTITUTION WILL BECOME A TRAINING GROUND FOR NEGRO LABORERS WHO WON'T JOIN LABOR UNIONS OR GO ON STRIKE, LIKE WHITE IMMIGRANTS...
... BECAUSE THE NEGRO HAS PROVEN HIMSELF TIME AND TIME AGAIN TO BE A LOYAL AND EFFECTIVE WORKER. IN TIMES OF SLAVERY, IF THE WHITE MAN NEEDED WORK DONE, HE KNEW HE COULD COUNT ON THE NEGRO. WHY SHOULD IT BE ANY DIFFERENT IN THESE GREAT TIMES OF CAPITAL AND INDUSTRY? IF YOU MAKE A DONATION TO TUSKEGEE I GUARANTEE YOU THAT IT WILL BE MONEY WELL SPENT.

MR. WASHINGTON, I'D LIKE TO MAKE A CONTRIBUTION.

127

THIS WAS THE FIRST TIME A BLACK PERSON HAD SPOKEN TO A LARGE CROWD OF PROMINENT SOUTHERN WHITES. THE ATLANTA COMPROMISE SPEECH GAVE WASHINGTON A LARGE WHITE FOLLOWING.

GREAT SPEECH, BOOKER.

WE NEED MORE NEGROES WITH YOUR ATTITUDE.

AND HE WAS REVERED BY RANK-AND-FILE BLACK PEOPLE.

MOMMA WANTS YOU TO GROW UP TO BE JUST LIKE BOOKER T.

BUT ONLY ONE YEAR AFTER THE ATLANTA COMPROMISE SPEECH, JIM CROW SEGREGATION CAME INTO FULL EFFECT WITH THE SUPREME COURT RULING OF PLESSY V. FERGUSON, STATING THAT " SEPARATE BUT EQUAL" WAS A REASONABLE INTERPRETATION OF THE FOURTEENTH AMENDMENT."

AT THE SAME TIME THAT WHITE AMERICA DEALT BLACK PEOPLE MAJOR POLITICAL SETBACKS, SUCH AS THE DEATH OF THE POPULIST MOVEMENT AND THE PLESSY V. FERGUSON DECISION, MANY WHITE PEOPLE DEVELOPED A FASCINATION WITH BLACK CULTURE.

THE 1890s SAW THE "CAKEWALK" SWEEP THE NATION.

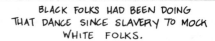

BLACK FOLKS HAD BEEN DOING THAT DANCE SINCE SLAVERY TO MOCK WHITE FOLKS.

AND THOSE WHITE CULTURE BANDITS STOLE OUR SONGS, TOO.

NO BODY KNOWS ♫ THE TRUBBLE I SEEN.

THOSE WHITE FOLKS SURE LIKE IMITATIN' BLACK FOLKS.

MAYBE WE SHOULD ACT LIKE WHITE FOLKS TREATING BLACK FOLKS WITH RESPECT. THAT WAY THE NEXT TIME THEY IMITATE US, WE'LL BE BETTER OFF.

AMEN TO THAT, SISTER.

WHILE SOME WHITE PEOPLE HARMLESSLY SANG AND DANCED TO BLACK RHYTHMS, OTHERS WERE WHISTLING TO A DIFFERENT, MURDEROUS TUNE.

STRING HIM UP.

SINCE THE MIDDLE OF THE 1600s, VIOLENCE HAD INTRUDED ON THE LIVES OF BLACK PEOPLE.

SPLASH!

INTRUDED! I'D SAY IT WAS A REGULAR VISITOR.

AT ANY RATE, IDA B. WELLS ADDRESSED THE ISSUE OF VIOLENCE HEAD ON.

DID YOU READ THAT LATEST ARTICLE BY IDA B. WELLS?

INDEED, I DID. YOU KNOW, SHE'S A SPUNKY WRITER, FOR A WOMAN.

SHE WAS A CRUSADER AGAINST LYNCHING, AND USED HER NEWSPAPER, THE MEMPHIS FREE SPEECH, AS HER PLATFORM.

131

The Memphis Free

THURSDAY MORNING, MARCH 10.

RIDDLED

The Mob's Summary Execution of the Three Negro Prisoners.

BUT IT WAS HER OUTRAGE OVER THE LYNCHING OF THREE SUCCESSFUL BLACK BUSINESSMEN IN MEMPHIS IN 1892 THAT MADE HER A LIFELONG ACTIVIST AGAINST LYNCHING.

AS A BUSINESSPERSON SHE WORKED TIRELESSLY TO BUILD HER NEWSPAPER. IN 1889, SHE CANVASSED THE DELTA REGION OF MISSISSIPPI, ARKANSAS, AND TENNESSEE TO BRING IN SUBSCRIPTIONS FOR THE <u>FREE SPEECH.</u>

AFTER THE LYNCHING, WELLS DEVELOPED HER OWN THEORY.

THE REASON FOR THE LYNCHING, MY FRIENDS, IS SIMPLE. THESE WERE BLACK MEN WHO DARED TO PROSPER, AND WHITE MEN WERE JEALOUS. LYNCHING IS A TOOL THAT WHITE FOLKS USE TO GET RID OF FINANCIALLY INDEPENDENT NEGROES.

AS WELLS SUBSTANTIATED HER BELIEF WITH RESEARCH, SHE USED HER NEWSPAPER TO DELIVER A CLEAR MESSAGE TO HER READERS.

FIVE CENTS.

We Negroes should save our money and leave this town which will neither protect our lives and property nor give us a fair trial in the courts.

I THINK IT'S HIGH TIME WE DO SOMETHIN' ABOUT THAT SMART-MOUTHED NIGRA WENCH...

WELLS'S FIERY WRITINGS DREW THE IRE OF SOME WHITE MEN.

GLUSH! GLUSH! GLUSH!

KEROSENE

THE MEMPHIS FREE SPEECH BUILDING WAS BURNED TO THE GROUND.

UNDAUNTED, SHE MOVED TO NEW YORK CITY AND BEGAN WORKING FOR A STALWART IN THE BLACK NEWSPAPER BUSINESS — T. THOMAS FORTUNE.

IDA, YOUR MISFORTUNE IS MY GOOD FORTUNE. I'M GLAD TO HAVE YOU AT THE NEW YORK AGE.

WELLS'S THOROUGH INVESTIGATION OF LYNCHING PRODUCED A FEATURE STORY ENTITLED "SOUTHERN HORROR LYNCH LAW IN ALL ITS PHASES." THE STORY GARNERED HER NATIONAL PROMINENCE.

BUT SHE WASN'T SATISFIED WITH BEING JUST A NATIONAL FIGURE.

1894: LONDON, ENGLAND

ONCE YOU CITIZENS OF ENGLAND LEARN OF THE ATROCITIES THAT YOUR AMERICAN COUSINS ARE COMMITTING AGAINST MY PEOPLE, I BELIEVE THAT YOU WILL FEEL COMPELLED TO HELP US.

The actions of Ida B. Wells prove that Negro women have no sense of virtue and are altogether without character.

BY 1896, NATIONALLY PROMINENT WHITES WERE GROWING IMPATIENT WITH WELLS' MILITANCY. THE PRESIDENT OF THE MISSOURI PRESS ASSOCIATION, IN AN EFFORT TO DISCREDIT HER, PUBLISHED A LETTER THAT DEFAMED WELLS AND ALL BLACK WOMEN.

THE LIBELOUS ATTACK BY THE MISSOURI PRESS ASSOCIATION BONDED MANY BLACK WOMEN TOGETHER, AND THE NATIONAL ASSOCIATION OF COLORED WOMEN WAS FORMED.

133

THE NACW BELIEVED IN DEALING WITH AMERICA'S RACE PROBLEMS BY AIDING BLACK WOMEN.
IT WAS LED BY MARY CHURCH TERRELL.

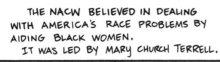

THE ASSOCIATION WAS MULTI-FACETED. IT DENOUNCED LYNCHING, BUT IT ALSO LOOKED FOR PRACTICAL SOLUTIONS TO THE PROBLEMS MARRIED BLACK WOMEN FACED.

UNLIKE MANY OF OUR WHITE COUNTER-PARTS, WE DO NOT HAVE THE LUXURY OF BEING ONLY HOUSEWIVES. WE MUST ALSO GO OUT AND WORK AT JOBS. IT IS WITH THAT IN MIND THAT THIS ORGANIZATION IS PROVIDING DAY NURSERIES FOR EMPLOYED MOTHERS.

AS TIME PROGRESSED, THE NACW BROADENED ITS SCOPE AND BECAME AN ORGANIZATION THAT ENHANCED THE LIVES OF MANY BLACK PEOPLE — MALE AS WELL AS FEMALE.

BUT TERRELL DID MORE THAN ORGANIZE. SHE WAS A BRILLIANT WOMAN WHO SPOKE THREE LANGUAGES FLUENTLY AND WAS ALSO AN EXCELLENT WRITER.

SHE CONSTANTLY WROTE ARTICLES ON THE NUMEROUS INJUSTICES BLACK PEOPLE FACED.

HAD WELLS AND TERRELL BEEN BORN IN A DIFFERENT TIME, THE CLARITY OF THEIR VISIONS WOULD HAVE ATTRACTED AN EVEN WIDER FOLLOWING. BUT IN THE 1890s, WHEN WOMEN OF ALL RACES WERE STILL DENIED THE RIGHT TO VOTE, THEIR BRILLIANCE WAS CLOUDED BY THE DOUBLE PREJUDICE THAT BLACK WOMEN WERE UP AGAINST.

NOT ONLY WERE MEN LIKE DR. GEORGE WASHINGTON CARVER INFLUENCED BY HIM, BUT HE WAS ALSO REVERED BY BLACK BUSINESS OWNERS.

IN 1900, WASHINGTON ORGANIZED THE NATIONAL NEGRO BUSINESS LEAGUE TO ENABLE BLACK BUSINESSMEN TO NETWORK AND MAKE CONTACTS.

TO WASHINGTON!

CLINK!

I'D LIKE TO PROPOSE A TOAST TO BOOKER T. WASHINGTON.

AS MEMBERS OF A UNITED LEAGUE OF BUSINESS MEN, YOU WILL FIND THAT YOUR PROFITS WILL SOAR.

BUT NOT EVERYONE WAS A FAN OF BOOKER T. WASHINGTON.

BOO!

BOOKER T. WASHINGTON IS THE BENEDICT ARNOLD OF THE NEGRO RACE!

1903 A NATIONAL NEGRO BUSINESS LEAGUE MEETING IN BOSTON.

MONROE TROTTER WAS JAILED FOR DISRUPTING AN NNBL MEETING.

BUT WASHINGTON'S MOST ARTICULATE CRITIC WAS W.E.B. DUBOIS.
FOR MORE THAN A DECADE DUBOIS HAD STUDIED AMERICA'S RACE PROBLEM.

DUBOIS CUT HIS INTELLECTUAL CHOPS IN 1897 AS A CHARTER MEMBER OF THE AMERICAN NEGRO ACADEMY — AN ALL-MALE ORGANIZATION FOUNDED BY THE BLACK MINISTER, EDUCATOR, AND EMIGRATIONIST ALEXANDER CRUMMELL.

AS SCHOLARS WE MUST PUBLISH AND DISTRIBUTE OUR OWN IDEAS, AND NOT IMITATE WHITE MEN.

IN 1903, HE TOOK HIS OWN ADVICE AND WROTE ONE OF THE CLASSICS OF BLACK LITERATURE, THE SOULS OF BLACK FOLK.

THE MAJESTY OF HIS WORDS CHALLENGED MANY FORMALLY EDUCATED BLACK PEOPLE TO ACTION — INCLUDING GEORGE EDWIN TAYLOR, WHO IN 1904 BECAME THE NATION'S FIRST BLACK PRESIDENTIAL CANDIDATE, THE NOMINEE OF THE ALL-BLACK NATIONAL LIBERTY PARTY.

NATIONAL LIBERTY PARTY
GEORGE EDWIN TAYLOR FOR PRESIDENT

NEVER BEFORE IN THE HISTORY OF AMERICAN NEGRO CITIZENSHIP HAS THE TIME BEEN SO OPPORTUNE FOR AN INDEPENDENT POLITICAL MOVEMENT ON THE PART OF THE RACE.... WHENEVER THE RACE AND THEIR CO-LABORERS SHALL ARRAY THEMSELVES IN ONE GRAND POLITICAL PHALANX THE VERY FOUNDATION OF THE TWO DOMINANT POLITICAL PARTIES SHALL BE SHAKEN....

THERE NEVER WAS A PRESIDENT GEORGE EDWIN TAYLOR, AND THE NATIONAL LIBERTY PARTY WOUND UP ON HISTORY'S SCRAP HEAP.
BUT ONE CAN ONLY WONDER WHAT WOULD'VE HAPPENED IF THE NATIONAL LIBERTY PARTY HAD CAUGHT ON.

WELCOME
TO BOLEY
ALL MEN UP
NOT
SOME MEN DOWN

AROUND 1890, MANY BLACK PEOPLE MIGRATED TO THE OKLAHOMA TERRITORY.

IN 1891, A NEW YORK TIMES ARTICLE FUELED WHITE FEARS BY WARNING THAT THE BLACK MIGRATION WAS ACTUALLY A PLOT TO TAKE OVER THE TERRITORY AND START AN ALL-BLACK STATE.

THE REALITY WAS THAT BLACK PEOPLE WENT TO THE OKLAHOMA TERRITORY LOOKING FOR ECONOMIC OPPORTUNITY AND A POLITICAL VOICE.

BLACK AND RED SEMINOLES HAD BEEN RELOCATED THERE BEFORE 1890, BUT THAT'S A WHOLE 'NOTHER STORY.

WHILE MANY BLACK PEOPLE SAW A CONFLICT BETWEEN THE IDEAS OF WASHINGTON AND DUBOIS, BLACK PEOPLE IN THE SOUTHWEST PUT BOTH CONCEPTS INTO ACTION, STRIVING FOR BOTH ECONOMIC SELF-RELIANCE AND POLITICAL EMPOWERMENT.

THEY WERE LED BY MEN LIKE E.P. McCABE AND THOMAS HAYNES, THE FOUNDERS OF LANGSTON AND BOLEY. NEARLY TWENTY-FIVE BLACK TOWNS SPRUNG UP IN THE OKLAHOMA TERRITORY BY 1906.

STILL, THE IRRATIONAL WHITE FEARS OF A BLACK TAKEOVER PERSISTED, AND IN 1906 AN ALL-WHITE CONSTITUTIONAL CONVENTION WAS CREATED.

Territorial Legislature

BLACKS AND NATIVE AMERICANS ORGANIZED THEIR OWN CONVENTIONS TO PROTEST, BUT TO NO AVAIL.

IN 1907, THEODORE ROOSEVELT ADMITTED OKLAHOMA INTO THE UNION WITH AN ALL-WHITE LEGISLATURE.

IN SPITE OF THE ENFORCED SECOND-CLASS CITIZENSHIP, SOME TOWNS LIKE BOLEY THRIVED.

BUT OTHERS LIKE LANGSTON AND LIBERTY NEVER FULFILLED THEIR INITIAL PROMISE.

IN MAY OF 1909, THE NATIONAL NEGRO CONFERENCE WAS CALLED TO ORDER.
THE NAME WAS A BIT MISLEADING, BECAUSE MANY LIBERAL WHITES ALSO ATTENDED.

... EVERY INTELLIGENT PERSON KNOWS THAT THE MOST PRESSING PROBLEM OF ANY PEOPLE SUDDENLY EMANCIPATED FROM SLAVERY IS THE PROBLEM OF REGULAR WORK AND ACCUMULATED PROPERTY.
BUT THIS PROBLEM OF WORK AND PROPERTY IS NO SIMPLE THING.... IT IS OFTEN SAID, "LET THE NEGROES ORGANIZE THEIR OWN THEATERS, TRANSPORT THEIR OWN PASSENGERS, ORGANIZE THEIR OWN INDUSTRIAL COMPANIES"; BUT SUCH KINDS OF BUSINESSES ARE ALMOST ABSOLUTELY DEPENDENT ON PUBLIC LICENSE AND TAXATION REQUIREMENTS.
A THEATER BUILT AND EQUIPPED COULD ONLY BY A SINGLE VOTE BE REFUSED A LICENSE. THIS IS NOT ALWAYS DONE BUT IT IS DONE JUST AS SOON AS ANY WHITE MAN OR GROUP OF WHITE MEN BEGIN TO FEEL THE COMPETITION.
POLITICAL POWER IS AN INDISPENSABLE PART OF ECONOMIC DEVELOPMENT.

WHILE DUBOIS WORKED FOR ADVANCEMENT THROUGH GROUP ACTION AND THE NAACP ESTABLISHED CHAPTERS IN BLACK COMMUNITIES THROUGHOUT THE COUNTRY, SOME BLACK PEOPLE ADVANCED BY SHEER DETERMINATION, INTELLIGENCE, AND BOUNDLESS ENERGY.

MADAME C.J. WALKER HAD ALL THAT AND THEN SOME. BY 1910 SHE WAS THE FIRST SELF-MADE MILLIONAIRESS IN AMERICA. BUT HER ROAD TO RICHES WAS FULL OF BUMPS AND POTHOLES.

She was born Sarah Breedlove in Louisiana in 1868. By the age of 15 she was a widow and a mother.

For more than two decades, she experienced the excruciating hardships familiar to most black people but especially to black women. In order to support herself and her child, she worked at all types of odd jobs.

She was poor, uneducated, and unskilled, but very, very smart.

Here's your laundry, Miss Jones.

Thank you, Sarah, and here's an extra two cents for your trouble.

I gotta find a better way than this.

What's wrong with your hair, Ma?

She was an innovative woman. After trying some off-the-shelf scalp treatments, she created her own— and it worked. But she didn't stop there.

MADAME WALKER'S HAIR CARE SYSTEM

Since many black women of her day suffered from scalp problems, she decided to establish her own business to sell her treatment. So she moved to Denver, Colorado, and with the help of her new husband, she sold the Walker Hair Care System to black women throughout the country.

BY 1912, SHE HAD ESTABLISHED A BUSINESS EMPIRE BASED IN INDIANAPOLIS, INDIANA, WHICH ENABLED HUNDREDS OF BLACK WOMEN TO BE SELF-SUFFICIENT AS SALESPEOPLE.

MR. WASHINGTON, WE KEEP RECEIVING MAIL FROM A MADAME C.J. WALKER. IT SEEMS THAT SHE'D LIKE TO BE A SPEAKER AT THE NEXT BUSINESS LEAGUE CONFERENCE.

THE HAIR WOMAN? COME NOW, MY CONFERENCE IS FOR BLACK CAPTAINS OF INDUSTRY, NOT HAIRDRESSERS.

1912: THE NATIONAL NEGRO BUSINESS LEAGUE CONVENTION. BOOKER T. WASHINGTON GIVES HIS FINAL STATEMENTS.

IF ANYONE IN THE AUDIENCE WOULD LIKE TO ASK QUESTIONS, NOW'S THE TIME.

BUT SEXIST BLACK BUSINESSMEN WOULDN'T GIVE HER HER PROPERS, EVEN THOUGH SHE WAS MORE SUCCESSFUL THAN ANY TEN OF THEM.

I HAVE A QUESTION.

THEN PLEASE STAND AND SPEAK.

I AM A WOMAN WHO CAME FROM THE COTTON FIELDS OF THE SOUTH. I WAS PROMOTED FROM THERE TO THE WASHTUB. THEN I WAS PROMOTED TO THE COOK KITCHEN, AND FROM THERE I PROMOTED MYSELF INTO THE BUSINESS OF MANUFACTURING HAIR GOODS AND PREPARATIONS. I HAVE BUILT MY OWN FACTORIES ON MY OWN GROUND. MY NAME IS MADAME C.J. WALKER, AND MY QUESTION IS, WHAT MORE MUST I DO TO BE RECOGNIZED AS A BUSINESS LEADER, **MISTER WASHINGTON?**

THE NEXT YEAR, MADAME WALKER WAS THE KEYNOTE SPEAKER OF THE NATIONAL NEGRO BUSINESS LEAGUE.

MADAME C.J. WALKER WAS JUST ONE OF MANY BLACK PEOPLE WHO ACHIEVED THEIR GOALS IN THE FACE OF EXTREME RESISTANCE.

MAGGIE LENA WALKER BECAME THE FIRST WOMAN BANK PRESIDENT IN AMERICA IN 1903.

I'M HAPPY TO SAY YOUR LOAN HAS BEEN APPROVED.

ROBERT ABBOT STARTED THE CHICAGO DEFENDER NEWSPAPER IN 1905.

CARTER G. WOODSON BECAME THE FATHER OF BLACK STUDIES IN 1915 BY STARTING THE ASSOCIATION FOR THE STUDY OF NEGRO LIFE AND HISTORY.

THE HISTORY OF THE NEGRO MUST BE DOCUMENTED AND TOLD.

BUT WHITE FOLKS TRIED NEW WAYS TO MAKE US LOOK LIKE A BUNCH OF FOOLS:

NO! NO! NO! IF I TOLD YOU ONCE, I TOLD YOU A THOUSAND TIMES, NIGRAS DON'T SAY "THIS" AND "THAT" THEY SAY "DIS" AND "DAT."

AND NEXT TIME ROLL YOUR EYES MORE.

IN 1915, A KENTUCKY RACIST NAMED D.W. GRIFFITH FILMED THE BIRTH OF A NATION, A MOVIE ABOUT THE FORMATION OF THE KU KLUX KLAN AFTER RECONSTRUCTION. THE KLAN WAS PORTRAYED AS A HEROIC ORGANIZATION. DESPITE ITS RACIST REPRESENTATIONS THIS MOVIE IS CONSIDERED A MASTERPIECE.

A MASTERPIECE OF TRASH.

WE DIDN'T TAKE THAT MESS LYIN' DOWN. THE NAACP PROTESTED TO PREVENT THE FILM FROM BEING SHOWN.

BIRTH OF A NATION IS AN ABOMINATION!

OUR PROTEST FAILED. BUT WHITES FROM ALL WALKS OF LIFE SAW THAT SOME OF US WOULD GIVE NO QUARTER.

THESE NEGROES ARE GETTING JUST A LITTLE TOO UPPITY.

ON NOVEMBER 4, 1915, THE GREAT BOOKER T. WASHINGTON DIED.

THESE NIGGERS WERE HARD ENOUGH TO DEAL WITH WHILE HE WAS ALIVE, NOW DUBOIS AND THOSE RADICALS ARE GONNA BE IMPOSSIBLE.

147

AFTER WASHINGTON'S DEATH, WHITE RACISM GREW MORE BRAZEN.

NOVEMBER 26, 1915: FULTON COUNTY, GEORGIA.

THE KU KLUX KLAN IS NOW OFFICIALLY REGISTERED IN THE GREAT STATE OF GEORGIA. HERE'S YOUR CHARTER, KEEP UP THE GOOD WORK.

THANK YOU, SIR.

A GOOD MANY WHITE AMERICANS WERE FOCUSED ON SPREADING HATE, BUT MANY BLACK PEOPLE ROSE ABOVE IT.

JULY 25, 1916: CLEVELAND WATERWORKS TUNNEL NUMBER 5. AFTER AN UNDERGROUND EXPLOSION, 12 MEN TRAPPED IN THE TUNNEL FOUGHT FOR THEIR LIVES AGAINST TOXIC FUMES.

COUGH, COUGH! I DON'T KNOW HOW MUCH LONGER I CAN HOLD ON.

MEANWHILE, ABOVE GROUND...

MEN ARE TRAPPED DOWN THERE, WE'VE GOT TO DO EVERYTHING IN OUR POWER TO SAVE THEM.

YEAH, BUT WHAT HELP CAN A NIGGER POSSIBLY BE?

LOOK, I DON'T HAVE TIME TO ARGUE WITH YOU. MR. MORGAN, YOU SAY THAT MASK OF YOURS PROTECTS AGAINST POISONOUS GAS?

THAT'S RIGHT.

SHUV!

WOULD YOU BE WILLING TO USE IT TO HELP SAVE THOSE TRAPPED MEN?

THAT'S WHY I'M HERE, SIR.

THREE.

YOU GOT ANY EXTRAS?

I NEED THREE MEN TO HELP MR. GARRET MORGAN GO DOWN AND RESCUE THOSE FELLAS.

WE'LL GO!

148

NATIONAL SAFETY DEVICE COMPANY

AFTER HIS HEROIC RESCUE IN THAT TUNNEL, GARRET A. MORGAN RECEIVED MUCH-NEEDED PUBLICITY FOR HIS GAS MASK AND WAS ABLE TO FORM THE NATIONAL SAFETY DEVICE COMPANY TO SELL IT.

BUT WHEN SOME FOLKS LEARNED HE WAS BLACK, MANY ORDERS WERE CANCELLED.

IN 1917, THE UNITED STATES OF AMERICA ENTERED WORLD WAR I, AND AMERICAN INVOLVEMENT RAISED AN OLD QUESTION IN THE BLACK COMMUNITY.

WE SHOULD BE FIGHTING AGAINST WHITE FOLKS, NOT FOR THEM.

THIS WAR IS FOR DEMOCRACY. IF WE, THE SONS AND DAUGHTERS OF AFRICA, ACQUIT OURSELVES WELL, THEN I BELIEVE WE SHALL HAVE JUSTICE AND EQUALITY IN THIS LAND. WE SHOULD CLOSE RANKS WITH OUR FELLOW AMERICANS.

THOUGH I FREQUENTLY DISAGREE WITH DR. DUBOIS, I DO BELIEVE HE IS CORRECT THIS TIME.

WITH ENCOURAGEMENT FROM BLACK LEADERS LIKE W.E.B. DUBOIS AND IDA B. WELLS, BLACK MEN REGISTERED TO FIGHT FOR THEIR COUNTRY IN WORLD WAR I.

MEANWHILE, WAR WAS STILL BEING WAGED ON BLACK PEOPLE IN AMERICA— 64 WERE LYNCHED IN 1916 ALONE.

MAY 1917: EAST ST. LOUIS, ILLINOIS

SINCE THE WHITE AMERICAN POPULATION WAS SO MUCH LARGER THAN THE BLACK AMERICAN POPULATION, WHITE PARTICIPATION IN THE WAR LEFT A SUBSTANTIAL LABOR SHORTAGE IN CITIES LIKE EAST ST. LOUIS.

TO HELP EASE THE LABOR SHORTAGE, MANY OUT-OF-WORK BLACK PEOPLE WERE BROUGHT IN TO FILL THE GAPS.

IN EAST ST. LOUIS, WHITE PEOPLE GREW RESENTFUL.

JULY 1, 1917

SOME OF OUR BOYS GO OFF AND FIGHT, AND THEY BRING IN NIGGERS TO DO OUR JOBS! IT'S TIME WE SHOW THEM NIGGERS A THING OR TWO.

POP!

POP!

LATER THAT DAY, THE BLACK COMMUNITY TALKED ABOUT SELF-DEFENSE.

ALL WE'RE TRYING TO DO IS EARN AN HONEST DOLLAR TO FEED OUR FAMILIES AND THE WHITE FOLKS ARE STILL TRYIN' TO KILL US.

ALL I KNOW IS THE NEXT TIME THEY ROLL THROUGH HERE WE'LL HAVE SOMETHIN' FOR 'EM!

WHILE THE BLACK COMMUNITY TALKED OF SELF-DEFENSE, EAST ST. LOUIS DEPLOYED PLAINCLOTHES POLICE TO CHECK ON THEM.

THE SARGE SAYS WE SHOULD ROLL THROUGH HERE TO KEEP AN EYE ON THE NIGGERS. HE SAYS THEY MIGHT BE PLANNIN' SOMETHIN'.

HEY, WHAT ARE YOU BOYS DOING THERE?

WHEN THE SMOKE CLEARED, A WHITE COP WAS DEAD. THE WHITE COMMUNITY OF EAST ST. LOUIS WENT ON A KILLING SPREE.

FOR THE NEXT TWO DAYS IT WAS OPEN SEASON ON BLACK PEOPLE.

BAM!

AT THE END OF THE RIOT, AT LEAST FORTY BLACK PEOPLE AND EIGHT WHITE PEOPLE WERE DEAD, AND $400,000 WORTH OF PROPERTY OWNED BY BLACK PEOPLE WAS DESTROYED.

AFTER THE TRAGEDY IN EAST ST. LOUIS, THE UBIQUITOUS W.E.B. DUBOIS PLANNED A RESPONSE TO THE VIOLENCE.

THOUGH WE CANNOT OUTFIGHT WHITE RACISM, WE MUST EXPRESS OUR INDIGNATION IN NO UNCERTAIN TERMS.

ON JULY 28, 1917, ON NEW YORK'S FIFTH AVENUE, DR. W.E.B. DUBOIS LED A PARADE OF 10,000 BLACK PEOPLE TO PROTEST THE CARNAGE IN EAST ST. LOUIS.

YET DESPITE THE ATROCITIES OF AMERICAN RACISM, MORE THAN TWO MILLION BLACK PEOPLE SERVED VALIANTLY AT HOME AND ABROAD IN WORLD WAR I.

IN FRANCE, HENRY JOHNSON AND NEEDHAM ROBERTS RECEIVED THE CROIX DE GUERRE, FRANCE'S HIGHEST MILITARY HONOR.

CORPORAL FREDDY STOWERS WAS RECOMMENDED FOR THE CONGRESSIONAL MEDAL OF HONOR FOR LEADING A CHARGE AGAINST GERMAN TROOPS.

HE RECEIVED IT POSTHUMOUSLY IN 1991, BUT THAT'S ANOTHER STORY.

AT CAMP GRANT ILLINOIS, BLACK RED CROSS NURSES WORKED 'ROUND THE CLOCK AT THE BASE HOSPITAL TO CARE FOR RETURNING VETERANS.

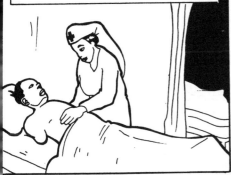

ON THE ECONOMIC FRONT, BLACK PEOPLE PURCHASED MORE THAN $250 MILLION WORTH OF WAR BONDS AND STAMPS.

I WANT A THOUSAND-DOLLAR BOND, AND I'LL PAY CASH FOR IT.

WHEN THE WAR ENDED IN 1919, BLACK PEOPLE HAD GIVEN IT EVERYTHING THEY HAD, AND WERE HOPEFUL THAT THIS TIME THEIR EFFORTS WOULD USHER IN AN ERA OF EQUALITY IN AMERICA.

WISHFUL THINKING...

THE YEAR THAT WWI ENDED WAS ONE OF THE BLOODIEST YEARS IN AMERICAN HISTORY.

IN 1919 THERE WERE MORE THAN 27 RACE RIOTS, AS WHITE RACISTS TRIED TO RE-ESTABLISH DOMINANCE OVER RETURNING BLACK SOLDIERS.

MORE JIM CROW LAWS WERE PASSED.

OOF!

SELF RELIANCE

BUT EVEN AFTER THAT "RED SUMMER" OF 1919, BLACK FOLKS...

... ATTENDED BASEBALL GAMES IN RUBE FOSTER'S NEWLY FORMED NATIONAL NEGRO BASEBALL LEAGUE...

... FOUND GAINFUL EMPLOYMENT WITH THE HELP OF GEORGE EDMOND HAYNES' NATIONAL LEAGUE ON URBAN CONDITIONS AMONG NEGROES,

COMMONLY KNOWN AS THE "NATIONAL URBAN LEAGUE"...

..."STOMPED THE BLUES" IN PLACES LIKE KANSAS CITY, MEMPHIS, AND HARLEM...

... AND ENROLLED IN COLLEGES, SUCH AS HOWARD, LINCOLN, AND ATLANTA UNIVERSITIES, THAT THEY OFTEN BUILT WITH THEIR OWN HANDS, AS WELL AS WITH FUNDS FROM WHITE PHILANTHROPISTS.

NEGROES HAD MUCH TO BE PROUD OF, AND NOBODY WAS MORE AWARE OF THAT THAN A JAMAICAN IMMIGRANT LIVING IN HARLEM NAMED MARCUS GARVEY.

GARVEY'S AMERICAN SOJOURN BEGAN IN HARLEM IN 1916 WHEN HE STARTED HIS BLACK NATIONALIST ORGANIZATION: THE UNIVERSAL NEGRO IMPROVEMENT ASSOCIATION.

AT FIRST, THE UNIA'S MEMBERSHIP WAS MADE UP PRIMARILY OF OTHER WEST INDIANS.

BUT DURING THE WAR YEARS GARVEY'S MESSAGE OF BLACK PRIDE AND HIS SENSE OF SHOWMANSHIP BEGAN TO HAVE WIDE APPEAL AMONG THE EVERYDAY PEOPLE OF HARLEM, AND WITH SOME PROMINENT BLACKS LIKE IDA B. WELLS.

THE IRISH HAVE IRELAND, THE CHINESE HAVE CHINA, I SAY AFRICA FOR THE AFRICANS – AT HOME AND ABROAD.

UP, YOU MIGHTY RACE, DO WHAT YOU MUST!

TELL IT MAHN!

BUT GARVEY WAS MUCH MORE THAN AN ORATOR AND SHOWMAN. HE WAS A MAN OF ACTION. BY 1920 THE UNIA HAD SEVERAL AUXILIARY ORGANIZATIONS.

THERE WAS THE BLACK NURSES' CORPS,

THE UNIVERSAL AFRICAN LEGION,

AND THE **NEGRO WORLD** NEWSPAPER.

157

BUT THE CROWNING GLORY OF THE UNIA WAS THE BLACK STAR STEAMSHIP LINE. WITH THIS FLEET OF STEAMSHIPS GARVEY PLANNED TO SET UP TRADE ROUTES BETWEEN AMERICAN BLACK-OWNED BUSINESSES AND AFRICA.

THE ARRAY OF THE UNIA'S ENTERPRISES AND THE FORCE OF GARVEY'S VISION ELECTRIFIED A LARGE SEGMENT OF BLACK AMERICA, AND WHEN A CROWD OF TWENTY-FIVE THOUSAND PEOPLE CAME TO HEAR GARVEY SPEAK AT NEW YORK'S MADISON SQUARE GARDEN, IT WAS CLEAR GARVEY HAD ARRIVED.

NOT ALL BLACK PEOPLE WERE ENAMORED WITH GARVEY. W.E.B DUBOIS WAS HIS MOST UNRELENTING CRITIC.

DR. DUBOIS, THE GARVEY MOVEMENT IS GROWING DAY BY DAY.

MOVEMENT, HA! IT IS TOO BOMBASTIC AND IMPRACTICABLE TO BE CALLED SUCH. NEGROES WILL SOON SEE IT FOR WHAT IT IS.

A FEW MONTHS LATER...

SO WHAT'S DUBOIS GOT TO SAY 'BOUT YOU MAHN?

"THE GARVEY MOVEMENT IS MORE STYLE THAN SUBSTANCE. IT REMAINS TO BE SEEN IF HE IS COMMITTED TO THE PEOPLE OR MERELY A RACIAL CON MAN."

NEEDLESS TO SAY, GARVEY DID NOT TAKE DUBOIS'S WORDS LIGHTLY.

DUBOIS IS A HALF-BREED ELITIST AND WISHES HE WERE WHITE.

158

WHAT SHOULD HAVE BEEN AN INTELLIGENT AND MEANINGFUL DIALOGUE BETWEEN TWO BRILLIANT MEN DEGENERATED INTO A NAME-CALLING CLASH OF EGOS.

AND SOON GARVEY WOULD HAVE MORE PROBLEMS THAN CHARACTER ASSASSINATIONS FROM DUBOIS.

IN 1922, MARCUS GARVEY WAS CONVICTED OF MAIL FRAUD AND SENTENCED TO PRISON. SOME PEOPLE SAY THAT DUBOIS AND HIS ASSOCIATES SET GARVEY UP, OTHERS SAY IT WAS J. EDGAR HOOVER AND THE FBI, WHILE STILL OTHERS SAY THAT IT WAS GARVEY'S QUESTIONABLE FINANCES THAT LED TO HIS DEMISE. BUT WHATEVER YOU BELIEVE, ONE FACT IS IRREFUTABLE. THE CLASH OF EGOS MARKED A LOW POINT IN BLACK LEADERSHIP.

AS THE GARVEY MOVEMENT SUNK, ANOTHER HARLEM-BASED MOVEMENT ROSE.

159

IN THE MID 1920S HARLEM WAS THE LARGEST BLACK URBAN COMMUNITY IN THE WORLD, AND THE ENERGY THAT EMANATED FROM IT FUELED A CULTURAL MOVEMENT KNOWN AS THE "HARLEM RENAISSANCE."

WHILE THE GARVEY MOVEMENT WAS ABOUT BLACK POWER, THE HARLEM RENAISSANCE WAS ABOUT BLACK EXPRESSION.

THE RENAISSANCE FEATURED AN EXPLOSION OF CREATIVITY BY WRITERS LIKE LANGSTON HUGHES, RUDOLPH FISHER, JESSIE FAUSET, NELLA LARSEN, ZORA NEALE HURSTON AND JEAN TOOMER.

RATHER THAN IMITATE WHITE ARTISTS, THEY ALL LOOKED FOR WAYS TO DEFINE BLACK AMERICAN CULTURE HOWARD UNIVERSITY PHILOSOPHY PROFESSOR ALAIN LOCKE CALLED THIS "THE EMERGENCE OF THE NEW NEGRO."

THE NEW NEGRO

THE CREATIVITY OF THE RENAISSANCE AFFECTED WHITE PEOPLE AS WELL AS BLACK.

ARE YOU READING SHAKESPEARE, DEAR?

HEAVENS NO, I'M READING COUNTEE CULLEN. HE'S ALL THE RAGE.

OF COURSE SOME WHITE PEOPLE'S INTEREST IN THE RENAISSANCE HAD A LOT TO DO WITH FINANCIAL GAIN,...

Cotton Club

... WHILE OTHERS SOUGHT PURELY "EXOTIC" AND "PRIMITIVE" ENTERTAINMENT, AND FAILED TO RECOGNIZE SERIOUS ART.

160

ALTHOUGH THE LATE 1920S SAW THE FLOWERING OF BLACK CREATIVITY, IT ALSO SAW A DEATH OF BLACK JOBS.

LEROY, I WON'T BE NEEDING YOU AT THE FACTORY ANYMORE.

WHAT?

THE FACTORY DOESN'T NEED YOU ANYMORE.

CAN YOU AT LEAST LET ME FINISH OUT THE DAY?

I'M AFRAID NOT.

ECONOMIC RECESSION

GARVEY MOVEMENT

HARLEM RENAISSANCE

BLACK BUSINESS DEVELOPMENT

THE PUNDITS THOUGHT THE RECESSION THAT ROCKED THOUSANDS OF BLACK FOLKS WAS JUST A BYPRODUCT OF THE MODERN TECHNOLOGICAL AGE.

GREAT DEPRESSION OF 1929

RRRRRRRRR

SO MUCH FOR THE PUNDITS...

161

WHEN THE GREAT DEPRESSION OF 1929 HIT, MILLIONS OF FOLKS, BOTH BLACK AND WHITE, FOUND THEMSELVES PENNILESS.

IT HIT WHITE FOLKS REAL HARD, BUT IT HIT BLACK FOLKS EVEN HARDER, AND THOUGH THEY TOOK PRIDE IN THE ACCOMPLISHMENTS OF THE 1920S, THAT PRIDE WASN'T PUTTING FOOD IN THEIR STOMACHS.

WHAT YOU READIN' THERE, BUDDY?

AN ESSAY BY PROFESSOR ALAIN LOCKE.

DOES HE SAY WHEN THESE HARD TIMES GONNA END?

NO, IT'S CALLED "THE NEW NEGRO." IT'S ABOUT HOW WE NEGROES ARE CHANGING OUR SELF-PERCEPTION.

HMMM, I'LL TELL YOU SOMETHIN', BUDDY. YOU AND YOUR PROFESSOR FRIEND MIGHT BE "NEW NEGROES," BUT YOU'RE LIVIN' IN THE SAME OLD AMERICA.

162

THE APPEALS TO RACE PRIDE THAT EARLIER HELPED BLACK BUSINESSES GROW COULDN'T OVERCOME THE FACT THAT MOST BLACK-OWNED BUSINESSES WERE JUST NOT EQUIPPED TO EMPLOY LARGE NUMBERS OF PEOPLE.

IF WE DO BUSINESS WITH OUR OWN, WE CAN GET OUT OF THIS DEPRESSION.

HEY, BUDDY, I DON'T KNOW WHAT WORLD YOU'RE LIVIN' IN, BUT YOU NEED MONEY TO DO BUSINESS WITH SOMEBODY.

AS THE ECONOMIC OUTLOOK FOR THE NATION GREW HORRIFYINGLY WORSE, MANY PEOPLE WERE FORCED TO LIVE IN MAKESHIFT SHANTY TOWNS CALLED "HOOVERVILLES" IN HONOR OF PRESIDENT HERBERT HOOVER.

TO COMBAT THE DEPRESSION'S DARK DAYS, GROUPS LIKE THE YOUNG NEGROES' COOPERATIVE LEAGUE IN HARLEM, LED BY ELLA BAKER, EXPLORED THE IDEA OF SELF-HELP THROUGH CONSUMER COOPERATION.

NONE OF US HAVE MUCH, BUT WE CAN BEAT THESE HARD TIMES BY POOLING OUR RESOURCES IN BUYING CLUBS, COOPERATIVE GROCERY STORES, AND DISTRIBUTION NETWORKS.

THOUGH CONSUMER COOPERATION WAS A NOBLE TACTIC, IT WAS NO MATCH FOR THE GREAT DEPRESSION.

FOOM!

WHO YOU GONNA VOTE FOR BABY, ROOSEVELT OR HOOVER?

ROOSEVELT, MOST LIKELY.

ROOSEVELT! HOW COULD YOU POSSIBLY VOTE DEMOCRAT? THEY THE ONES THAT DID ALL THE JIM CROW SEGREGATION. HELL, IF IT WASN'T FOR THE REPUBLICANS AND LINCOLN WE'D STILL BE PICKIN' COTTON.

FOR YOUR INFORMATION, A LOT OF US ARE STILL PICKIN' COTTON. IF WE WAIT FOR HOOVER AND YOUR REPUBLICANS TO DO SOMETHING, COLORED FOLKS'LL BE NOTHING BUT SKIN AND BONES.

I TELL YA, THEY SHOULD'VE NEVER GAVE WOMEN THE VOTE BACK IN 1920.

YOU THINK SO, HUH? WELL DON'T LET THAT ROOSEVELT "NEW DEAL" JAZZ FOOL YA. THE PARTY OF LINCOLN'LL FIX THIS DEPRESSION.

GO AHEAD AND THINK THAT, BUT I'M GONNA TURN THAT PICTURE OF LINCOLN TO THE WALL AND VOTE FOR ROOSEVELT.

THE SUNNY TIME
VOL 1
ROOSEVELT
!!!!.... WINS

DESPITE DEBATES LIKE THAT IN BLACK COMMUNITIES ACROSS THE COUNTRY, HOOVER GOT TWO-THIRDS OF THE BLACK VOTE IN 1932. NONETHELESS, ROOSEVELT WON THE ELECTION AND AMERICA PREPARED ITSELF FOR A NEW ADMINISTRATION AND A "NEW DEAL."

WHEN FDR TOOK OFFICE, HE PROMISED A NEW DEAL. BUT THE RESULTS FOR BLACK PEOPLE WERE MIXED. THE FEDERAL EMERGENCY RELIEF ADMINISTRATION AND OTHER RELIEF PROGRAMS HELPED BLACKS, BUT OFTEN IN SEGREGATED GROUPS OR WITH LESS GENEROUS RATIONS THAN IT PROVIDED FOR WHITES.

AND THE AGRICULTURAL ADJUSTMENT ADMINISTRATION UNWITTINGLY ENCOURAGED THE CORRUPTION INHERENT IN THE SHARE-CROPPING SYSTEM. MANY LANDLORDS TOOK ADVANTAGE OF ILLITERATE SHARE-CROPPERS AND STOLE LAND-GRANT CHECKS INTENDED TO HELP THEM.

I DON'T SEEM TO SEE A CHECK HERE FOR YOU.

THE MAN SAID HE SENT IT FOR ME.

YOU MUST HAVE HEARD HIM WRONG.

AS BLACK PEOPLE'S ECONOMIC WOES FAILED TO IMPROVE, W.E.B. DUBOIS QUESTIONED THE STRATEGIES OF THE NAACP.

VOTING RIGHTS AND ENDING SEGREGATION ARE EXTREMELY IMPORTANT, BUT OUR PEOPLE ARE LITERALLY **STARVING**. WE MUST PLACE MORE EMPHASIS ON ECONOMICS. WE COULD TAKE STEPS IN THAT DIRECTION BY ENCOURAGING THAT OUR PEOPLE SPEND WHAT LITTLE MONEY THEY HAVE THESE DAYS WITH ONE ANOTHER. A FORM OF VOLUNTARY ECONOMIC SEGREGATION, IF YOU WILL.

YOU SOUND LIKE BOOKER T. WASHINGTON, BURGHARDT. ECONOMIC SEGREGATION, EVEN IF IT IS VOLUNTARY, WILL ENCOURAGE WHITE PEOPLE TO INTENSIFY RACIAL DISCRIMINATION.

BUT DISCRIMINATION **HAS** INTENSIFIED OVER THE LAST TWENTY-FIVE YEARS, EVEN AS WE ATTEMPTED TO BATTLE IT. I'M MERELY SUGGESTING A WAY FOR NEGROES TO WORK TOGETHER TO END OUR DIRE FINANCIAL STRAITS. WE KNOW WHITE PEOPLE WON'T HELP US WITH THAT.

IF WE ENCOURAGE SEGREGATION IT WILL SPREAD LIKE A CANCER.

THAT'S WRONG. IF WE ENCOURAGE ECONOMIC COOPERATION AMONG OURSELVES, ALL WILL BENEFIT. BESIDES, IF WE ARE NOT WILLING TO HELP ONE ANOTHER, WHAT MAKES YOU THINK THE MAJORITY OF WHITE PEOPLE WILL BE WILLING TO HELP US?

DUBOIS AND WALTER WHITE NEVER CAME TO AN AGREEMENT, AND ON JULY 1, 1934, W.E.B DUBOIS RESIGNED FROM THE NAACP, AN ORGANIZATION HE HAD BEEN INSTRUMENTAL IN CONCEIVING AND BUILDING.

IN THE MID-1930s, DUBOIS WASN'T THE ONLY PERSON LOOKING FOR A CHANGE IN THE STRATEGIES OF BLACK ORGANIZATIONS. IN DETROIT, W.D. FARD AND ELIJAH MUHAMMAD CARRIED ON THE SELF-RELIANCE WORK OF THE NATION OF ISLAM.

MEANWHILE THE CHICAGO-BASED NATIONAL MOVEMENT FOR THE ESTABLISHMENT OF A 49TH STATE THOUGHT THAT AN ALL-BLACK STATE WOULD BE THE ANSWER TO BLACK PEOPLE'S PROBLEMS.

AND IN HARLEM, FATHER DIVINE'S PEACE MISSION MOVEMENT ATTRACTED MANY NEGROES WHOSE ECONOMIC POSITION WAS SOMEWHAT LESS THAN COMFY.

TRUST IN ME AND GOD WILL PROVIDE.

FOR THE FIRST TIME SINCE SLAVERY, BLACK FOLKS BEGAN TO QUESTION AMERICA'S ENTIRE ECONOMIC SYSTEM.

WHAT YOU READIN' NOW, PROFESSOR?

KARL MARX'S "DAS KAPITAL." HE ARGUES THAT CAPITALISM IS THE CAUSE OF OUR PROBLEMS.

THAT MIGHT BE THE CAUSE OF YOUR PROBLEMS, BUT I THINK **WHITE FOLKS** ARE THE CAUSE OF MINE.

1935: HARLEM. ADAM CLAYTON POWELL JR. ADDRESSES A PICKET LINE.

BY 1935 3 MILLION OF THE 18 MILLION PEOPLE RECEIVING RELIEF WERE BLACK.

IT SEEMED FRANKLIN DELANO ROOSEVELT'S PROGRAMS GENUINELY REDUCED THE SUFFERING OF MANY BLACK PEOPLE.

WE WILL BOYCOTT AND PICKET THE PHONE COMPANY, THE LIGHT COMPANY, THE BUS COMPANY, THE WORLD'S FAIR, AND THE DIME STORES AND DEPARTMENT STORES UNTIL THE RESIDENTS OF HARLEM RECEIVE A FAIR SHAKE IN THE WORK FORCE.

BY BUILDING ON THE WORK BEGUN IN 1933 BY THE CITIZEN'S LEAGUE FOR FAIR PLAY, THE "BUYING POWER" MOVEMENT HELPED GIVE MORE THAN ONE THOUSAND NEW JOBS TO HARLEM RESIDENTS OVER A FOUR-YEAR SPAN.

BUT IT WAS LIKE A REPLAY OF RECONSTRUCTION, BECAUSE THIS WAS MAINLY RELIEF IN THE FORM OF FOOD AND SHELTER.
WHEN IT CAME TO JOBS, HELP WASN'T AS FORTHCOMING, SO WE HAD TO HELP OURSELVES.

AT THE SAME TIME, A. PHILIP RANDOLPH, WHO IN 1925 FORMED THE BROTHERHOOD OF SLEEPING CAR PORTERS AND MAIDS, LOOKED TO CHANNEL THE BLOSSOMING ENERGY OF BLACK PROTEST INTO A NEW ORGANIZATION— THE NATIONAL NEGRO CONGRESS.

TRUE LIBERATION CAN BE ACQUIRED ONLY WHEN THE NEGRO PEOPLE POSSESS POWER; AND POWER IS THE PRODUCT AND FLOWER OF ORGANIZATION: ORGANIZATION OF THE MASSES, THE MASSES IN THE MILLS AND MINES, ON FARMS, IN FACTORIES, IN CHURCHES, IN FRATERNITIES, IN HOMES, COLLEGES, WOMEN'S CLUBS, STUDENT GROUPS, TRADE UNIONS, TENANT'S LEAGUES, COOPERATIVE GUILDS, POLITICAL ORGANIZATIONS, AND CIVIL RIGHTS ASSOCIATIONS.

BUT DESPITE RANDOLPH'S GRAND VISION, THE NATIONAL NEGRO CONGRESS HAD INTERNAL PROBLEMS.

THE ORGANIZATION IS GROWING. SOON WE CAN ORGANIZE THE BLACK PROLETARIAT AND OVERTHROW THE OPPRESSOR. REVOLUTION IS NEAR AND LIBERATION WILL BE OURS.

A. PHILIP RANDOLPH

OUR PEOPLE NEED MONEY, NOT REVOLUTION.

SURELY THAT CANNOT BE THE AIM OF OUR ORGANIZING. REVOLUTION IS INEVITABLE.

OVER TIME, THE COMMUNIST ARGUMENT WON OUT AND A. PHILIP RANDOLPH LEFT THE NATIONAL NEGRO CONGRESS. IT FLOUNDERED, BUT HE WOULD BE HEARD FROM AGAIN.

MEANWHILE, AMERICA WAS STILL AMERICA.

GET UP OUTTA THAT SEAT SO MY FRIEND CAN SIT DOWN!

1936: BERLIN OLYMPICS

HUF! PUF!

YOU SEE, AS LONG AS JESSE OWENS WAS RUNNING RACES OVERSEAS, HE WAS A HERO, BUT WHEN HE RETURNED TO AMERICA'S SHORES, HE WAS JUST ANOTHER NIGGER. IN ORDER TO MAKE A LIVING, HE WAS REDUCED TO DEMEANING EXHIBITIONS LIKE RACING AGAINST HORSES.

LATER...

OUR BOY JESSE KICKED THOSE GERMANS' BUTTS.

YEAH, IT MAKES YOU PROUD TO BE PART OF THE RED, WHITE, AND BLUE.

FOUR GOLD MEDALS— FOR THIS!

BUT NOT ALL WHITE PEOPLE WERE INSENSITIVE TO THESE INJUSTICES.
IN FACT, ELEANOR ROOSEVELT WAS ONE OF THE STAUNCHEST ADVOCATES BLACK PEOPLE HAD.

FRANKLIN, YOU NEED TO DO MORE TO GIVE NEGROES AN EQUAL OPPORTUNITY.

I'M DOING AS MUCH AS I CAN ALREADY. WHAT MORE CAN I DO?

CLINK!
BOODLE.

WELL, FOR STARTERS, YOU COULD INVOLVE NEGRO LEADERS IN DECISIONS THAT AFFECT THEIR PEOPLE.
TAKE MY FRIEND MARY McLEOD BETHUNE, FOR INSTANCE —

I'M SURE SHE COULD BENEFIT YOUR ADMINISTRATION GREATLY.

FOLLOWING THE FIRST LADY'S ADVICE, FDR CREATED A "BLACK CABINET" IN HIS SECOND TERM TO ADVISE THE ADMINISTRATION ON RACE ISSUES.

THE CABINET'S LEADER WAS THE GREAT MARY McLEOD BETHUNE.
DECADES EARLIER SHE HAD FOUNDED BETHUNE-COOKMAN COLLEGE.
AS A DIRECTOR OF MINORITY AFFAIRS FOR THE NATIONAL YOUTH ADMINISTRATION, SHE WORKED DILIGENTLY TO CREATE OPPURTUNITIES FOR HER PEOPLE.

169

AS HARD AS BLACK LIFE WAS IN THE LATE 1930S, BLACK PEOPLE STILL FOUND INNOVATIVE FORMS OF **RE-CREATION.** WHETHER IT WAS ROCKING TO THE MUSIC OF COUNT BASIE AND LESTER YOUNG...

..... OR THE GREAT DUKE ELLINGTON AND HIS COLLABORATOR, COMPOSER BILLY STRAYHORN, WHO WERE POSSIBLY THE GREATEST AMERICAN-BORN MUSICAL COMPOSERS OF THAT- OR ANY-DAY ...

... CHEERING ON THEIR MAN JOE LOUIS...

... WATCHING THEIR FAVORITE NEGRO LEAGUE BALLPLAYERS IN PITTSBURGH'S BLACK-OWNED GREENLEE STADIUM...

... OR LISTENING TO THE JOKES OF JACKIE "MOMS" MABLEY, BLACK FOLKS WENT ON LIVING, LAUGHING, AND STRIVING AGAINST STEEP ODDS.

170

THE CREATIVITY AND RESILIENCE OF BLACK CULTURE GOT BLACK FOLKS THROUGH THE TENUOUS 1930s, BUT THE 1940s PRESENTED NEW PROBLEMS, FOR THE ENTIRE WORLD.

IN 1941, ADOLF HITLER AND THE NAZIS CONTINUED THEIR DEMONIC RUN THROUGH EUROPE, AND SPREAD WAR ACROSS THE ENTIRE CONTINENT.

I TELL YA, THIS WAR'S GETTING SO BIG, IT'S ALL WE CAN DO JUST TO KEEP UP WITH DEMAND.

YEAH, WE'RE HIRIN' SO MANY MEN WE'RE RUNNIN' OUTTA SPACE.

I HEARD YOUR COMPANY IS HIRING.

I'M SORRY, WE JUST HIRED OUR LAST MAN.

THE AMERICAN ECONOMY WAS HEATING UP, YET NEGROES WERE STILL OUT IN THE COLD. HOWEVER, A. PHILIP RANDOLPH WAS NOT GOING FOR THAT DOUBLE STANDARD.

IT'S TIME OUR PEOPLE GET A PIECE OF THE PIE AND NOT JUST THE CRUST.

THAT'S EASIER SAID THAN DONE, PHIL.

LIKE FREDERICK DOUGLASS SAID, "NO STRUGGLE, NO PROGRESS."

AS LEADERS LIKE RANDOLPH AND ADAM CLAYTON POWELL FOUGHT FOR BLACK RIGHTS, AMERICA WAS ON ITS WAY TO WAR ONCE AGAIN.

DECEMBER 7, 1941: PEARL HARBOR

ONCE AGAIN, BLACK PEOPLE ANSWERED AMERICA'S CALL TO WAR IN SPITE OF THE SECOND-CLASS-CITIZEN STATUS IMPOSED UPON THEM.

WE STILL HADN'T LEARNED OUR LESSON.

WHEN THE JAPANESE BOMBED PEARL HARBOR, DORIE MILLER, A BLACK COOK ON ONE OF THE AMERICAN SHIPS DOCKED THERE, TOOK CONTROL OF A MACHINE GUN AND SHOT DOWN FOUR JAPANESE AIRPLANES. AFTER THE BOMBING, AMERICAN INVOLVEMENT IN WORLD WAR II OFFICIALLY BEGAN.

... AND ENGAGED IN COMBAT IN THE EUROPEAN THEATER.

MORE THAN 500,000 BLACK TROOPS SAW OVERSEAS SERVICE IN SEGREGATED FORCES.

THEY SERVED IN PORT BATTALIONS...

AMMUNITION

BATTALIONS LIKE THE 614th AND THE 333rd MADE A DIFFERENCE ON EUROPEAN SOIL AT CLIMBACH AND BRITTANY.

IN THE PACIFIC, THE 93rd DIVISION FOUGHT VALIANTLY UNDER ADVERSE TROPICAL CONDITIONS, WHILE BLACK MARINES DEFENDED SEVERAL STRATEGIC OUTPOSTS.

THE 761st TANK BATALLION HELPED RESCUE THE VICTIMS OF GERMAN RACISM IN CONCENTRATION CAMPS AT BUCHENWALD AND DACHAU...

GOOD GOD!

... AND THE 99th PURSUIT SQUADRON, MORE COMMONLY REFERRED TO AS THE TUSKEGEE AIRMEN, MADE THEIR MARK ESCORTING ALL-WHITE BOMBER CREWS OVER EUROPE DURING THE WAR. THEY DIDN'T LOSE ONE BOMBER.

WE HAVE AN ENEMY PLANE AT 3 O'CLOCK.

AND INDIVIDUALS LIKE COL. BENJAMIN O. DAVIS AND CAPTAIN CHARLES L. THOMAS HELPED AMERICA WIN NUMEROUS BATTLES.

WE SHOULD INVADE HERE.

THESE BRAVE SOULS SAW THE HORRIBLE RESULT OF HATRED AND BRUTALITY.

1945: NEW YORK CITY

THURGOOD MARSHALL CONVENES A HIGH-LEVEL NAACP MEETING.

GENTLEMEN, WITH THE WAR NOW OVER, IT'S TIME WE REEVALUATE OUR TACTICS IN COMBATING SEGREGATION.

IN WHAT WAY? WE'VE BEEN SUCCESSFUL IN COMBATING SEGREGATION ALREADY. WHY, LOOK AT THE SUPREME COURT'S DECISION IN GAINES V. MISSOURI. WE HAD THAT YOUNG MAN ADMITTED TO LAW SCHOOL.

YES, BUT HIS CASE WAS EXCEPTIONAL. OUR PRIMARY AIM IS TO END SEGREGATION BY ATTACKING JIM CROW EDUCATION.
THE SLICK SOUTHERNERS PROVIDE BETTER FUNDING FOR SEPARATE NEGRO SCHOOLS IN ORDER TO AVOID INTEGRATION.

I'M NOT SURE I'M FOLLOWING YOUR LOGIC, MARSHALL. ISN'T FUNDING FOR OUR OWN SCHOOLS DESIRABLE?

NOT IF IT MEANS THAT THOSE SCHOOLS ARE THE **ONLY** CHOICES AVAILABLE TO OUR PEOPLE.

BUT DON'T YOU THINK WE COULD BE DOING DAMAGE TO THE SCHOOLS THAT NOW SERVE OUR PEOPLE? MAYBE SOME STUDENTS WILL BENEFIT FROM INTEGRATED SCHOOLS, BUT WHAT OF THE BLACK TEACHERS AND ADMINISTRATORS? DO YOU THINK INTEGRATED INSTITUTIONS WILL OPEN THEIR DOORS TO HIRE THEM?

YOU'LL HAVE TO HAVE FAITH THAT IN A TRULY DEMOCRATIC NATION, THE PRINCIPLES OF DEMOCRACY WILL BENEFIT ALL PEOPLE.

WAH! YAH! CRAK! SEGRE GATION SEGRE GATION

BLACK FOLKS HAD DONE A REMARKABLE JOB OF INSTITUTION-BUILDING DURING THE MOST BITTER JIM CROW TIMES. BUT AFTER THE MEETING IN 1945, THE NAACP DECIDED TO FOCUS ITS EFFORTS ON DISMANTLING SEGREGATION RATHER THAN BUTTRESSING THE "EQUAL" IN "SEPARATE BUT EQUAL."

177

FOR ALL OF THE NAACP'S EFFORTS, THE BIRTH OF MODERN AMERICAN INTEGRATION OCCURRED ON A BASEBALL DIAMOND, WHEN JACKIE ROBINSON PLAYED HIS FIRST GAME FOR THE BROOKLYN DODGERS ON APRIL 10, 1947.

BEFORE ROBINSON BEGAN PLAYING WITH THE DODGERS, THE NATIONAL NEGRO LEAGUE CONSISTENTLY OUTDREW THE MAJOR LEAGUES IN LARGE AMERICAN CITIES LIKE NEW YORK AND CHICAGO.
BUT ONCE ROBINSON WAS ASSIMILATED INTO THE MAJORS, OTHER BLACK TALENT BEGAN HEADING TO THE MAJORS.

THEREAFTER THE NEGRO LEAGUES ALL BUT DISAPPEARED—ONE OF MANY BLACK INSTITUTIONS LOST TO INTEGRATION.

ALONG WITH JACKIE ROBINSON, BLACK WOMEN AND MEN CHALLENGED THE RACIAL STATUS QUO IN WAYS THAT WERE NEVER SEEN BEFORE.

WILLIAM HASTIE, A FORMER MEMBER OF ROOSEVELT'S BLACK CABINET, WAS APPOINTED JUDGE OF THE THIRD U.S. CIRCUIT COURT OF APPEALS.

IN 1952, RALPH ELLISON WROTE <u>INVISIBLE MAN</u>, A BOOK MANY CONSIDER THE BEST AMERICAN NOVEL EVER.

THAT SAME YEAR, CHARLOTTA SPEARS BASS CO-FOUNDED THE PROGRESSIVE PARTY AND RAN FOR VICE-PRESIDENT OF THE UNITED STATES.

WIN OR LOSE, WE WIN BY RAISING THE ISSUES!

IN 1954, PERCY LAVON JULIAN, A CHEMIST WORLD RENOWNED FOR HIS CORTISONE RESEARCH, STARTED JULIAN LABORATORIES, INC.

BUT THE APOGEE OF THOSE ACHIEVEMENTS WAS REACHED LATER THAT YEAR WHEN THURGOOD MARSHALL FINALLY DEFEATED LEGAL SEGREGATION BY WINNING THE CASE OF BROWN V. BOARD OF EDUCATION OF TOPEKA, KANSAS, WHICH CALLED FOR DESEGREGATION OF AMERICA'S SCHOOLS.

SEGREGATION IS A SYSTEM OF DEPRIVATIONS IMPOSED ON THE NEGRO.

TO THE CONTRARY, SEGREGATION DOES NOT DEPRIVE THE NEGRO, IT SHIELDS HIM FROM COMPETITION WITH BETTER PREPARED AND BETTER QUALIFIED WHITE STUDENTS.

SUPREME COURT CHIEF JUSTICE EARL WARREN SUMMARIZED HIS DECISION.

IN THE FIELD OF PUBLIC EDUCATION THE DOCTRINE OF SEPARATE BUT EQUAL HAS NO PLACE.... SEPARATE EDUCATIONAL FACILITIES ARE INHERENTLY UNEQUAL.

THROUGHOUT THE SOUTH, WHITE CITIZENS COUNCILS STEPPED UP THEIR ACTIVITIES TO FIGHT DESEGREGATION.

AS GOD IS MY WITNESS, MY KIDS AIN'T GOING TO NO SCHOOL WITH NIGRAS IN IT.

AUGUST 24, 1955: MONEY, MISSISSIPPI

AND THE RACISM DIDN'T STOP THERE.

HOW YOU DOIN, MISS?

THAT NIGGER SASSED THE WRONG WOMAN.

FOUR DAYS LATER...

WHITE FOLKS MAIMED AND LYNCHED FOURTEEN-YEAR-OLD EMMETT TILL FOR WHAT THEY CALLED "RECKLESS EYEBALLING." THE TWO MEN THAT WERE CHARGED WITH HIS MURDER WERE ACQUITTED BY AN ALL-WHITE JURY.

YET IN THE FACE OF THAT WICKEDNESS, BLACK FOLKS WERE BUILDING A JUGGERNAUT FOR EQUALITY. FROM 1949 TO 1955, A BLACK WOMEN'S ORGANIZATION KNOWN AS THE WOMEN'S POLITICAL COUNCIL PLANNED TO PROTEST THE SEGREGATED BUSES OF MONTGOMERY, ALABAMA.

WOMENS POLITICAL COUNCIL

LADIES, I BELIEVE WE'RE READY.

WHEN ONE OF ITS MEMBERS, ROSA PARKS, REFUSED TO MOVE TO THE BACK OF THE BUS, THE GRITS HIT THE PAN AND THE WOMEN'S **POLITICAL** COUNCIL HELPED MOBILIZE MONTGOMERY'S BLACK COMMUNITY IN A CITYWIDE BUS BOYCOTT.

BLACK PEOPLE CARPOOLED, RODE MULES, AND WALKED TO WORK.

HOW MANY MORE DAYS WE GOT TO WALK? MY FEET ARE KILLING ME.

VROOOOOM!

I DON'T KNOW ABOUT YOU, BUT IF HURT FEET IS THE PRICE I GOT TO PAY TO GET WHITE FOLKS TO TREAT ME LIKE A HUMAN BEING, THEN THAT'S ONE BILL I'M WILLIN' TO PAY, WITH INTEREST!

BUOYED BY A YOUNG **BAPTIST** MINISTER NAMED MARTIN LUTHER KING, JR., THEY STAYED OFF OF MONTGOMERY'S BUSES FOR MORE THAN A YEAR.

NOT ONLY HAVE THE BUS COMPANIES' PROFITS BEEN CUT BY TWO-THIRDS, BUT WE HAVE OBSERVED THAT OUR OWN NEGRO SHOPS ARE THRIVING BECAUSE WE ARE FINDING IT INCONVENIENT TO WALK DOWNTOWN TO THE WHITE STORES. WE HAVE A NEW RESPECT FOR THE PROPER USE OF OUR DOLLAR.

IN DECEMBER 1956, THE SUPREME COURT DECLARED ALABAMA'S SEGREGATED BUSES UNCONSTITUTIONAL. THE BOYCOTTERS HAD WON AND MARTIN LUTHER KING WAS CATAPULTED TO THE NATIONAL STAGE.

IN JANUARY OF 1957, KING FOUNDED A NEW PROTEST ORGANIZATION, THE SOUTHERN CHRISTIAN LEADERSHIP CONFERENCE.

WE NOW KNOW THAT THE SOUTHERN NEGRO HAS COME OF AGE, POLITICALLY AND MORALLY.

BUT THE IMAGE OF A TRIUMPHANT BLACK PROTEST RUBBED MANY WHITES THE WRONG WAY.

TURN THE DAMN CHANNEL! I'M GETTIN' TIRED OF THOSE PEOPLE.

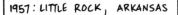

1957: LITTLE ROCK, ARKANSAS

A WHITE BACKLASH KICKED IN AS WHITE FOLKS TRIED TO PREVENT THE INTEGRATION OF CENTRAL HIGH SCHOOL.

GO BACK WHERE YOU CAME FROM!

SEND THOSE JUNGLE BUNNIES BACK TO AFRICA!

THE STUDENTS ATTENDED CENTRAL THAT YEAR, BUT THE SCHOOL WAS SHUT DOWN A YEAR LATER.

THIS AINT THE LAST YOU HEARD FROM US.

IN CONGRESS, STROM THURMOND FILIBUSTERED AGAINST CIVIL RIGHTS LEGISLATION GUARANTEEING EQUAL RIGHTS FOR BLACKS. THAT WINDBAG KEPT THE SENATE FROM MOVING ON ANY LEGISLATION FOR 24 HOURS.

DESPITE THE WHITE BACKLASH, TELEVISION MADE BLACK PEOPLE MORE VISIBLE AND IN SOME WAYS MORE ACCEPTABLE TO MAIN STREET, U.S.A.

THOSE NEGROES ARE REALLY QUITE TALENTED, YOU KNOW.

BUT IN 1959, TELEVISION SHOWED MAIN STREET A DIFFERENT TYPE OF BLACK PERSON, WHEN CBS AIRED A SPECIAL ENTITLED "THE HATE THAT HATE PRODUCED." IN IT, AMERICA WAS INTRODUCED TO THE NATION OF ISLAM AND ITS UNCOMPROMISING NATIONAL SPOKESMAN, MALCOLM X.

I DON'T KNOW, THAT ONE LOOKS PRETTY MEAN TO ME.

THE HONORABLE ELIJAH MUHAMMAD TEACHES US THAT THE WHITE MAN IS THE DEVIL, AND THAT THE ONLY HOPE FOR THE SO-CALLED NEGRO IS TO SEPARATE HIMSELF FROM THE WHITE MAN AND DO FOR HIMSELF.

SAVIOR IS BORN

READ THE WORDS OF ALLAH'S LAST MESSENGER, THE HONORABLE ELIJAH MUHAMMAD.

THE NATION OF ISLAM WAS LARGELY A NORTHERN PHENOMENON. IT TAPPED MANY OF THE SAME INTENSE EMOTIONS THAT GARVEY TAPPED FORTY YEARS EARLIER, BUT UNLIKE GARVEY'S MORE UNIVERSAL PHILOSOPHY, THE ZEALOUS RELIGIOUS DOCTRINE OF THE NOI LIMITED ITS APPEAL TO SEGMENTS OF BLACK AMERICA,

MEANWHILE, IN GREENSBORO, NORTH CAROLINA, A GROUP OF COLLEGE STUDENTS DEMANDED TO BE SERVED AT A WOOLWORTH'S LUNCH COUNTER.
A FEW MONTHS AFTER THE WOOLWORTH'S SIT-IN A DYNAMIC NEW ORGANIZATION WAS FOUNDED: THE STUDENT NONVIOLENT COORDINATING COMMITTEE. ITS PRINCIPAL ARCHITECT WAS THE BRILLIANT LONGTIME ACTIVIST ELLA BAKER.

WE'RE NOT MOVING TILL WE GET SOME COFFEE.

THAT SAME YEAR, IN PHILADELPHIA, BLACK MINISTERS ORGANIZED A BOYCOTT OF SUN OIL, GULF OIL, TASTEE BAKING AND PEPSI-COLA, RESULTING IN THE HIRING OF 600 BLACKS IN ADMINISTRATIVE AND MANAGERIAL POSITIONS.

BLACK CONSUMER POWER WAS NOTICED BY SOME ON WALL STREET.

1961: THE BOARDROOM OF THE PEPSI-COLA CORPORATION

GENTLEMEN, AS YOU CAN SEE FROM THE RESULTS OF THE ROPER REPORT ON NEGRO CONSUMER PREFERENCES AND ATTITUDES, WE HAVE OUR WORK CUT OUT FOR US IF WE WANT TO PENETRATE THE NEGRO MARKET.

TO HELP ACCELERATE THIS PROCESS, I HAVE PROMOTED HARVEY C. RUSSELL TO THE POSITION OF VICE PRESIDENT OF SPECIAL MARKETS.

AT THE SAME TIME, AN AMBITIOUS BLACK-OWNED DETROIT RECORD COMPANY CALLED MOTOWN SET ITS SIGHTS ON THE EAR-DRUMS OF YOUNG BLACK AND WHITE AMERICANS.

SOUNDS LIKE A WINNER TO ME, BABY.

SNAP!

AS THE MOTOWN SOUND STARTED TO SWEEP THE PEPSI GENERATION, A NEW FORM OF PROTEST DEVELOPED — **THE FREEDOM RIDE.**

IT WASN'T NEW. THE CONGRESS OF RACIAL EQUALITY HAD DONE SIMILAR THINGS BACK IN '47 TO CHALLENGE JIM CROW LAWS ON AMERICA'S BUSES. HUF! PUFF! A COALITION OF BLACK AND WHITE COLLEGE STUDENTS WORKING PEACEFULLY TOGETHER FOR CHANGE — THAT WAS WHAT AMERICA WAS SUPPOSED TO BE ABOUT.

NOT EVERYBODY WAS IMPRESSED BY THE RIDES...

WHAT GOOD IS IT TO RIDE ON AN INTEGRATED BUS IF YOU DON'T HAVE BUS FARE?

BUT FOR ALL HIS INSIGHT AND WIT MALCOLM WAS STILL A NORTHERNER AND DID NOT FULLY GRASP THE RISK RUN BY ANY FORM OF PROTEST IN THE SOUTH.

WAITING AREA WHITES ONLY

THAT'S WHAT I THINK OF YOUR FREEDOM RIDE.

BUT MEDGAR EVERS DID. AS A FIELD WORKER FOR THE NAACP, EVERS WAS DEEPLY INVOLVED IN DESEGREGATING PUBLIC ACCOMODATIONS IN MISSISSIPPI.

FIGHT SEGREGATION

SOMEBODY NEEDS TO TEACH THAT BOY A LESSON.

YOU HAVE A RIGHT TO USE ANY PUBLIC FACILITY IN THIS STATE.

ON JUNE 12, 1963, MEDGAR EVERS WAS SHOT IN THE BACK AND KILLED BY A WHITE SUPREMACIST NAMED BYRON DE LA BECKWITH.

POW!

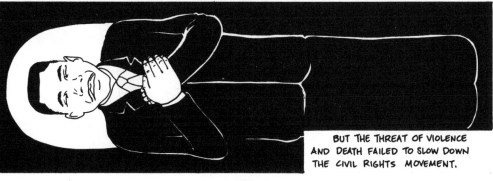

BUT THE THREAT OF VIOLENCE AND DEATH FAILED TO SLOW DOWN THE CIVIL RIGHTS MOVEMENT.

THAT SAME YEAR, BAYARD RUSTIN AND A. PHILIP RANDOLPH ORGANIZED A MARCH ON WASHINGTON. BUT THOUGH THEY PLANNED THE EVENT, MARTIN LUTHER KING, JR., WAS THE MARCH'S MOST COMPELLING FIGURE.

... THE NEGRO IS STILL LANGUISHING IN THE CORNERS OF AMERICAN SOCIETY AND FINDS HIMSELF AN EXILE IN HIS OWN LAND.... IN A SENSE WE HAVE COME TO OUR NATION'S CAPITAL TO CASH A CHECK. WHEN THE ARCHITECTS OF OUR REPUBLIC WROTE THE MAGNIFICENT WORDS OF THE CONSTITUTION AND THE DECLARATION OF INDEPENDENCE, THEY WERE SIGNING A PROMISSORY NOTE TO WHICH EVERY AMERICAN WAS TO FALL HEIR. INSTEAD OF HONORING THIS SACRED OBLIGATION, AMERICA HAS GIVEN THE NEGRO PEOPLE A BAD CHECK, A CHECK WHICH HAS COME BACK MARKED "INSUFFICIENT FUNDS." BUT WE REFUSE TO BELIEVE THE BANK OF JUSTICE IS BANKRUPT.... SO WE HAVE COME TO CASH THIS CHECK— A CHECK THAT WILL GIVE US UPON DEMAND THE RICHES OF FREEDOM AND THE SECURITY OF JUSTICE.

AFTER MARTIN LUTHER KING ROCKED THE NATION DURING THE MAGNIFICENT MARCH ON WASHINGTON FOR JOBS AND FREEDOM, PRESIDENT JOHN F. KENNEDY MADE THE STRONGEST STATEMENT AGAINST SEGREGATION EVER MADE BY A PRESIDENT.

BUT ON SEPTEMBER 15TH IN BIRMINGHAM, ALABAMA, ONE MONTH AFTER THE MARCH,

A BOMB EXPLODED IN THE SIXTEENTH STREET BAPTIST CHURCH...

SEGREGATION IS MORALLY WRONG. IT'S TIME TO ACT IN THE CONGRESS, IN YOUR STATE AND LOCAL LEGISLATIVE BODIES, AND IN ALL OF OUR DAILY LIVES TO END IT.

...KILLING ADDIE MAE COLLINS, DENISE McNAIR, CAROLE ROBERTSON, AND CYNTHIA WESLEY - FOUR YOUNG GIRLS ATTENDING SUNDAY SCHOOL THERE.

AND TWO MONTHS AFTER THE BIRMINGHAM BOMBING, JOHN F. KENNEDY WAS ASSASSINATED. AMERICA'S VIOLENCE WAS CATCHING UP WITH HER.

IN MEMORY OF

DENISE McNAIR   CYNTHIA WESLEY   ADDIE MAE COLLINS   CAROL ROBERTSON

THEIR LIVES WERE TAKEN BY UNKNOWN PARTIES ON SEPTEMBER 15, 1963 WHEN THE SIXTEENTH STREET BAPTIST CHURCH WAS BOMBED

"MAY MEN LEARN TO REPLACE BITTERNESS AND VIOLENCE WITH LOVE AND UNDERSTANDING"

PRESIDENT JFK 1917 - 1963

1964 WAS AN ELECTION YEAR, AND SPURRED BY THE EVENTS OF 1963, THE FEDERAL GOVERNMENT TOOK ACTION.

THE 24th AMENDMENT TO THE CONSTITUTION PROHIBITED THE USE OF POLL TAXES. THE POLL TAX WAS COMMONLY USED BY WHITES IN ALABAMA AND MISSISSIPPI TO DISENFRANCHISE BLACK VOTERS.

THE CIVIL RIGHTS ACT OF 1964 PROHIBITED DISCRIMINATION IN PUBLIC ACCOMODATIONS AND EMPLOYMENT.

HERE'S MY JOB APPLICATION. CAN YOU TELL ME WHERE YOUR RESTROOM IS?

AND THE ECONOMIC OPPORTUNITY ACT PROVIDED ONE BILLION DOLLARS FOR A GROUP OF PROGRAMS KNOWN AS THE "WAR ON POVERTY."

HeadStar

IT SHOULD HAVE BEEN BACK PAY FOR SLAVERY.

MEANWHILE, IN MISSISSIPPI, MAJOR MOVES WERE AFOOT.

FREEDOM SUMMER WAS THE BRAINCHILD OF SNCC IN CONJUNCTION WITH OTHER CIVIL RIGHTS ORGANIZATIONS INCLUDING CORE AND MARTIN LUTHER KING'S SCLC. TOGETHER THEY FORMED THE COUNCIL OF FEDERATED ORGANIZATIONS. THE LEADERS OF THIS NEW GROUP WERE BOB MOSES AND JAMES FORMAN.

THIS SUMMER PROJECT HAS THREE GOALS...

... TO START COMMUNITY CENTERS HERE IN MISSISSIPPI...

COMMUNITY CENTER LITERACY PROGRAM

... TO ESTABLISH FREEDOM SCHOOLS TO COMPLEMENT THE BASIC EDUCATION THAT THE PEOPLE HERE RECEIVE...

FREEDOM SCHOOL

... AND FINALLY, TO ESTABLISH A POLITICAL PLATFORM THAT WILL HELP REGISTER VOTERS AND LAUNCH THE MISSISSIPPI FREEDOM DEMOCRATIC PARTY. THIS PARTY WILL CHALLENGE THE SEATING OF THE REGULAR MISSISSIPPI DEMOCRATIC PARTY AT THE NATIONAL CONVENTION.

MS. HAMER, WE'RE GOING TO NEED YOUR HELP.

YOU HAVE IT.

BUT AS ACTIVISM INCREASED, SO DID THE BODY COUNT. THREE FREEDOM SUMMER VOLUNTEERS, ANDREW GOODMAN, JAMES CHANEY, AND MICHAEL SCHWERNER, WERE MURDERED BY WHITE RACISTS.

AUGUST 24, 1964: ATLANTIC CITY, NEW JERSEY. THE NATIONAL DEMOCRATIC CONVENTION

UNDAUNTED, THE FREEDOM WORKERS CONTINUED THEIR STRUGGLE, AND THE MISSISSIPPI FREEDOM DEMOCRATIC PARTY WAS READY TO MAKE ITS MOVE.

WE DIDN'T COME HERE TO SIT IN THE BACK SEAT OF THE CONVENTION.

FANNIE LOU HAMER

THE MFDP WAS NOT RECOGNIZED AS THE SOLE REPRESENTATIVE OF MISSISSIPPI DEMOCRATS AT THE CONVENTION. INSTEAD, A COMPROMISE WAS WORKED OUT BETWEEN THE OLD-GUARD CIVIL RIGHTS ORGANIZATIONS AND THE NATIONAL DEMOCRATIC PARTY. THE COMPROMISE, WHICH THE MFDP FOUND UNACCEPTABLE, GAVE THE MFDP TWO AT-LARGE SEATS ON THE CONVENTION FLOOR. MANY MFDP MEMBERS FELT MARTIN LUTHER KING, JR., AND THE MAINSTREAM CIVIL RIGHTS ORGANIZATIONS HAD SOLD THEM OUT.

GO BACK TO TREE SWINGING, YOU BLACK APES.

HAMER'S OPINION WAS A LITTLE OFF THE MARK. KING MAY HAVE HAD UTOPIAN DREAMS, BUT HE WAS ALSO A MAN OF CONVICTION AND COURAGE. IN 1965 HE ORGANIZED A MARCH IN ALABAMA, FROM SELMA TO MONTGOMERY. IT WAS A HAZARDOUS UNDERTAKING, BUT THE MARCHERS ALL SUBSCRIBED TO KING'S PHILOSOPHY OF NONVIOLENCE.

WHEN THE MARCHERS GOT TO MONTGOMERY THEY WERE JOINED BY 50,000 OTHER PEOPLE. TO SAY THE LEAST, THE MARCH WAS A SUCCESS. SOON THEREAFTER, PRESIDENT LYNDON JOHNSON SIGNED THE VOTING RIGHTS ACT OF 1965.

DON'T BE FOOLED. 1965 WASN'T ONLY ABOUT BLACK SUCCESSES AGAINST THE ODDS. EARLIER THAT YEAR, OUR BLACK SHINING PRINCE, MALCOLM X, WAS GUNNED DOWN WHILE GIVING A SPEECH IN HARLEM.

... AND OUR YOUNG MEN DIED IN DISPROPORTIONATE NUMBERS IN A QUESTIONABLE WAR TO CONTAIN COMMUNISM IN VIETNAM.

MEANWHILE, IN THE WATTS SECTION OF LOS ANGELES, A RIOT BROKE OUT AFTER A BLACK MAN WAS KILLED BY A WHITE POLICEMAN.

WATTS WAS BLACK ANGER INCARNATE. IN SPITE OF THE LEGISLATIVE GAINS, MOST BLACKS WERE STILL BEHIND THE EIGHT BALL. BY 1966, A NEW PHILOSOPHY CAME ON THE SCENE. IT WAS CALLED "BLACK POWER."

VIBRANT NEW ORGANIZATIONS LIKE THE BLACK PANTHER PARTY FOR SELF-DEFENSE ATTEMPTED TO EMPOWER IMPOVERISHED BLACK COMMUNITIES THROUGH RHETORIC AND COMMUNITY ORGANIZING.

THE FOOD IS FREE YOUNG BROTHER, EAT UP.

THE PANTHERS MAY HAVE BEEN ABOUT BREAKFAST PROGRAMS AND SELF-HELP IN PRIVATE, BUT ULTIMATELY THEIR GUN-TOTING PUBLIC PERSONA BROUGHT THEM DOWN.

THESE PEOPLE NEED TO BE STOPPED.

THEY HAD THEIR FAULTS, BUT NOBODY DENIED THAT THE PANTHERS IMAGE OF DEFIANCE AND STRENGTH BROUGH OUT THE BEST IN MANY OF US.

FOLKS LIKE RON KARENGA, AMIRI BARAK AND NIKKI GIOVANNI TOOK THAT BLACK POWE SPIRIT AND SPARKED AN INTEREST IN AFRIC HERITAGE BY FOUNDING KWANZAA AND TH BLACK ARTS MOVEMENT.

AND THEN THERE WAS MUHAMMAD ALI.

1967: THE DRAFT BOARD FOR THE VIETNAM WAR

WHY SHOULD I FIGHT IN VIETNAM? THE VIET CONG AIN'T CALLED ME NO NIGGER.

BY REFUSING TO FIGHT IN THE VIETNAM WAR, MUHAMMAD ALI HIGHLIGHTED AN AGE-OLD AMERICAN CONTRADICTION:
WHY SHOULD WE FIGHT IN AMERICA'S WARS WHILE AMERICA'S RACISTS WERE AT WAR WITH US?

WHY?

BECAUSE NOT ALL AMERICA WAS RACIST. IN 1967 IN THE MIDST OF THE BLACK POWER MOVEMENT, THE SUPREME COURT DECISION IN LOVING V. VIRGINIA LEGALIZED INTERRACIAL MARRIAGES IN THE SEVENTEEN STATES THAT BARRED THEM.

BUT THAT DECISION WAS LOST IN WHAT WAS KNOWN AS THE LONG HOT SUMMER. IN CITIES LIKE NEWARK, DETROIT, AND CLEVELAND, THOUSANDS OF BLACK PEOPLE RIOTED IN RESPONSE TO POLICE BRUTALITY, POOR HOUSING, AND UNEMPLOYMENT— ALL BYPRODUCTS OF AMERICAN RACISM.

AND THE EVENTS OF THE LONG HOT SUMMER AND THE VIETNAM WAR WERE NOT LOST ON DR. KING.
HIS ANALYSIS CONTINUED TO EXPAND AND MATURE.

AMERICA EXPLOITS PEOPLE OF COLOR AT HOME AND ABROAD. THE VIETNAM WAR IS WRONG.

NOT ONLY DID KING QUESTION VIETNAM BUT HE BEGAN TO CONFRONT THE ECONOMIC PROBLEMS OF POOR PEOPLE.

OUR IDEA IS TO DRAMATIZE THE WHOLE ECONOMIC PROBLEM OF THE POOR. JOBS ARE ON THE DECLINE AS A RESULT OF TECHNOLOGICAL CHANGE.... YET CONGRESS REFUSES TO GIVE US MORE WELFARE ASSISTANCE WHILE WE LOOK FOR JOBS. THEY CLAIM MORE WELFARE WOULD BE A HANDOUT. HANDOUTS TO THE RICH ARE GIVEN SOPHISTICATED NOMENCLATURE SUCH AS "PARITIES," "SUBSIDIES" AND "INCENTIVES TO INDUSTRY."

KING WAS ASSASSINATED BY JAMES EARL RAY IN 1968 IN MEMPHIS, TENNESSEE, WHILE HE WAS SUPPORTING A STRIKE OF BLACK SANITATION WORKERS.

THE VIOLENT DEATH OF A BELOVED LEADER ADDED TO AN ALREADY LONG LIST OF BLACK GRIEVANCES AND BROUGHT ON MORE RIOTING.

BAR

BEER WINE

PARKING ONE HOUR 7ᵃᵐ-6ᵖᵐ

194

OCTOBER 16, 1968: MEXICO CITY

BUT THE DEFINITIVE IMAGE OF BLACK PROTEST IN THE LATE 1960s WAS THE BLACK POWER SALUTE THAT TOMMIE SMITH AND JOHN CARLOS GAVE ON THE VICTORY STAND OF THE 1968 OLYMPICS.

KING'S MURDER AND THE SMITH-CARLOS PROTEST MARKED THE END OF AN ERA.

IN NOVEMBER 1968, RICHARD NIXON'S "LAW AND ORDER" CAMPAIGN LANDED HIM IN THE WHITE HOUSE.

BUT NIXON WASN'T ALL BAD. HIS ADMINISTRATION INVESTED FEDERAL RESERVE FUNDS IN BLACK-OWNED BANKS AND ENCOURAGED POLICIES OF BUSINESS HIRING AND SCHOOL ADMISSIONS THAT WOULD COME TO BE KNOWN AS "AFFIRMATIVE ACTION."

OOH!

WITH THE ADVENT OF AFFIRMATIVE ACTION PROGRAMS, MORE AND MORE BLACK FOLKS CLIMBED THE LADDER TO EXECUTIVE SUITES AND PROFESSORS' SEATS.

AFFIRMATIVE ACTION HELPED THE BLACK MIDDLE CLASS TO GROW, BUT FOR MANY OF US POVERTY WAS STILL THE ORDER OF THE DAY.

BUZ!

SO IN 1972, IN GARY, INDIANA, A NATIONAL BLACK POLITICAL CONVENTION WAS HELD TO LOOK FOR COMPREHENSIVE SOLUTIONS TO OUR PROBLEMS.

BUT BLACK PEOPLE DIDN'T JUST LOOK TO POLITICAL AGITATION FOR SOLUTIONS. WE ALSO FOUNDED PROFESSIONAL ORGANIZATIONS LIKE THE NATIONAL ASSOCIATION OF BLACK MBAs IN 1972, AND THE BLACK DATA PROCESSING ASSOCIATES IN 1975.

POWER TO THE PEOPLE

195

BY 1977, NIXON WAS OUT OF OFFICE, AND JIMMY CARTER WAS IN. CARTER APPOINTED MANY BLACK PEOPLE TO HIGH-LEVEL POSITIONS, INCLUDING CLIFFORD ALEXANDER AS SECRETARY OF THE ARMY.

MR. PRESIDENT, THIS LIST OF RECOMMENDATIONS FOR PROMOTIONS IS TOTALLY UNACCEPTABLE.

IN WHAT WAY?

QUITE FRANKLY, IT NEEDS TO INCLUDE MORE BLACK PEOPLE.

ALEXANDER SAW TO IT THAT MANY BLACK PEOPLE WERE PROMOTED TO THE UPPER ECHELONS OF THE ARMED FORCES. ONE OF THE BENEFICIARIES WAS COLIN POWELL, WHO WOULD GO ON TO BECOME HEAD OF THE NATIONAL SECURITY COUNCIL.

WHILE ALEXANDER WORKED AWAY FROM THE SPOTLIGHT, ALEX HALEY'S BOOK <u>ROOTS</u> WAS CAST UNDER IT. IT AIRED AS A TV MINI-SERIES THAT INSPIRED MILLIONS OF BLACK AND WHITE PEOPLE WITH HALEY'S STORY OF SLAVERY AND SUCCESS AGAINST THE ODDS.

BUT WHILE <u>ROOTS</u> GAVE SOME BLACK FOLKS A WARM FUZZY FEELING, THE RECESSION OF THE MID-1970s LEFT OTHERS OUT IN THE COLD.

WELL

THAT RECESSION WAS A HARBINGER OF THINGS TO COME. BY 1981, BLACK PEOPLE FACED A MAJOR CHALLENGE- THE RONALD REAGAN PRESIDENCY.

RAY-GUN SET THE TONE FOR HARD TIMES. HE PROPOSED LEGISLATION THAT WOULD RELIEVE THE PRESSURE AFFIRMATIVE ACTION PUT ON SMALL BUSINESSES TO HIRE MINORITIES AND WOMEN.

IN THE FACE OF REAGANOMICS, BLACK PEOPLE LOOKED FOR A POLITICAL FOOTHOLD. PEOPLE LIKE CONRAD WORRILL OF THE NATIONAL BLACK UNITED FRONT LOOKED TO BUILD INSTITUTIONS IN BLACK COMMUNITIES THROUGHOUT THE COUNTRY.

AND IN 1983, WITH THE HELP OF WORRILL AND OTHER BLACK NATIONALISTS, HAROLD WASHINGTON, A MODERATE DEMOCRAT, DEFEATED THE CHICAGO DEMOCRATIC POLITICAL MACHINE AND BECAME THAT CITY'S FIRST BLACK MAYOR.

AND IN 1984, JESSE JACKSON MADE A HIGHLY PUBLICIZED RUN FOR THE PRESIDENCY. HE LOST, BUT HIS RAINBOW COALITION HELPED ADD NEW VOTERS TO THE DEMOCRATIC PARTY ROLLS.

BUT BY THE MID 1980s, HOPE WAS A SCARCE COMMODITY IN MANY BLACK COMMUNITIES.

WHEN PHILADELPHIA'S MAYOR WILSON GOODE, A BLACK MAN, SANCTIONED THE BOMBING OF A BLACK BACK-TO-NATURE ORGANIZATION NAMED

MOVE

HE INDIRECTLY KILLED 11 BLACK PEOPLE AND DESTROYED THE HOMES AND PROPERTY OF BLACK WORKING-CLASS PEOPLE ON AN ENTIRE CITY BLOCK, IT SEEMED BLACK POLITICIANS DIDN'T ALWAYS HAVE BLACK PEOPLE'S INTERESTS IN MIND.

AFTER THE MOVE TRAGEDY, BLACK PROGRESS TOOK ON A DISTINCTLY INDIVIDUAL TONE.

IN 1987, REGINALD LEWIS BECAME THE FIRST BLACK MAN TO OWN AND OPERATE A FORTUNE 500 COMPANY— THE BEATRICE CORPORATION.

WHY SHOULD WHITE GUYS HAVE ALL THE _FUN_?

THAT SAME YEAR, DR. MAE JEMISON BECAME THE FIRST BLACK WOMAN ASTRONAUT IN THE U.S. SPACE PROGRAM.

AND IN 1989, PRESIDENT GEORGE BUSH NAMED COLIN POWELL THE CHAIRMAN OF THE JOINT CHIEFS OF STAFF. THIS WAS AT A TIME WHEN THE MILITARY WAS BECOMING THE MOST EGALITARIAN INSTITUTION IN AMERICA.

ALL THOSE YEARS OF DYING FOR AMERICA WERE FINALLY BEING RECOGNIZED.

THANK YOU, CLIFFORD.

BUT FOR EVERY COLIN POWELL MOVIN' ON UP, THERE WAS A RODNEY KING GETTING BEATEN ON DOWN.

YET IN THE FACE OF THOSE PROBLEMS, BLACK PEOPLE FOUND WAYS TO RE-CREATE. AT FESTIVALS LIKE THE INTERNATIONAL AFRICAN ARTS FESTIVAL IN BROOKLYN, THE BLACK ARTS FESTIVAL IN NORTH CAROLINA, THE ODUNDE FESTIVAL IN PHILADELPHIA, AND THE INDIANA BLACK EXPO, WE SHOWED PRIDE IN OUR HERITAGE AND CULTURE.

WHILE SPIKE LEE, TONI MORRISON, WYNTON MARSALIS, AND NUMEROUS HIP-HOP ARTISTS ILLUMINATED THE COMPLEXITY OF BLACK AMERICAN LIFE.

BUT CULTURAL PRIDE AND A SENSE OF BEAUTY HAVE THEIR LIMITATIONS. BY THE MID-1990s MORE THAN A MILLION BLACK PEOPLE LIVED IN ABJECT POVERTY — A POVERTY THAT COULD BE TRACED BACK TO THE POLICIES OF ANDREW JOHNSON'S RECONSTRUCTION.

THAT'S ONE THING WE BOTH AGREE ON.

NOW SHOWING

MEANWHILE, MANY AMERICANS CLAIMED THAT RACISM WAS DEAD AND THAT BLACK PEOPLE NEEDED TO STOP COMPLAINING AND START HELPING THEMSELVES.

PARADOXICALLY, OTHERS LIKE CHARLES MURRAY ARGUED THAT BLACK PEOPLE WERE INTELLECTUALLY INFERIOR TO WHITE PEOPLE.

SOUNDS LIKE RACISM IS ALIVE AND WELL TO ME.

THE BELL CURVE

BOOK SIGNING

SEEMS THE ONLY PEOPLE WHO HAVE CONSISTENTLY HELPED BLACK PEOPLE IN AMERICA HAVE BEEN OTHER BLACK PEOPLE.

IN THE LATE 1990s, BLACK PEOPLE REMAINED HOPEFUL AND DISTINCTLY DIVERSE. ESSAYISTS LIKE STANLEY CROUCH AND ALBERT MURRAY REFUTED RACIST DRIBBLE LIKE MURRAY'S BY MAINTAINING THAT BLACK CULTURE IS CENTRAL TO AMERICAN CULTURE...

WITHOUT NEGRO CULTURE, THERE IS NO AMERICAN CULTURE.

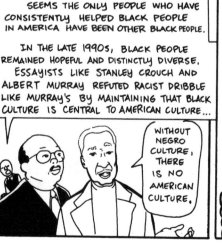

... WHILE SCHOLARS LIKE DR. MOLEFI ASANTE MAINTAIN THAT AFRICAN CULTURE IS CENTRAL TO WESTERN CIVILIZATION.

MANY OF THE ANCIENT GREEKS STUDIED IN AFRICA.

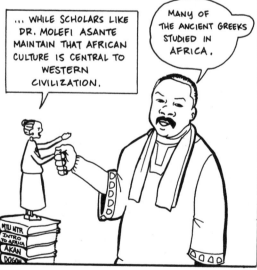

NTU NTR
INTRO TO AFRICA
AKAN
DOGON

IN EARLY 1995, THE MOST CONTROVERSIAL BLACK MAN IN AMERICA, NATION OF ISLAM LEADER LOUIS FARRAKHAN, HAD AN IDEA.

WE MUST HAVE A DAY FOR THE SPIRITUAL REBIRTH OF THE BLACK MAN.

AND WHEN HE SAID "THE BLACK MAN" HE MEANT THE BLACK MAN AND THE BLACK MAN ONLY.
HIS IDEA BECAME KNOWN AS THE "MILLION MAN MARCH" ON WASHINGTON, D.C.

NEEDLESS TO SAY, THE IDEA SET OFF A SIGNIFICANT STIR IN THE BLACK COMMUNITY.

THIS ISN'T THE 1960s — WHAT DO WE NEED A MARCH ON WASHINGTON FOR?
BESIDES, THAT FARRAKHAN IS A BLACK RACIST.

I DON'T KNOW ABOUT THAT, I JUST THINK BLACK WOMEN SHOULD PARTICIPATE TOO.

MOTHERLAND SPRING WATER

BUT THE IDEA OF A MARCH STRUCK A CHORD WITH MANY.

YOU GOIN' TO THE MARCH?

MOST DEFINITELY!

WHEN THE DAY CAME, BLACK MEN FROM ALL WALKS OF LIFE TRAVELED TO WASHINGTON, D.C., FOR THE MARCH.

ALL ABOARD FOR WASHINGTON!

204

205

207

AND WHO CAN FORGET HOW HE DID A MEDIA SUCKER PUNCH ON SISTER SOULJAH DURING HIS FIRST CAMPAIGN

MEDIA SUCKER PUNCH? SHE WAS WAY OUT OF LINE, THE WAY SHE TALKED ABOUT THE 1992 LA RIOTS.

TAP! TAP! TAP!

IT WAS A REBELLION... ANYWAY... IN 1999, THAT SAME SISTER SOULJAH WROTE A BOOK CALLED "THE COLDEST WINTER EVER".

HA HA HA HA HA !!

WHAT'S SO FUNNY?

YOU!

THIS BOOK HELPED BEGIN A NEW LITERARY MOVEMENT CALLED "STREET LITERATURE."

HAVE YOU LOST YOUR BLOOMIN' MIND? THAT'S HARDLY HISTORY, AND IT SURE ISN'T LITERARY.

OH REALLY. IF THE HARLEM RENAISSANCE IS HISTORY, IF THE BLACK ARTS MOVEMENT IS HISTORY, THEN SO IS STREET LITERATURE AND GOSPEL PLAYS FOR that matter... THEY REPRESENT OUR ORGANIC CULTURAL CREATIONS.

THANK YOU, BECAUSE DESPITE YOUR OVER CRITICAL OUTLOOK. THINGS HAVE GOTTEN BETTER FOR BLACK PEOPLE HERE. BY THE YEAR 2000 37% OF ALL BLACK PEOPLE WERE MIDDLE CLASS. IN 1970 ONLY 3% WERE, AND NOW THERE ARE OVER 10,000 BLACK ELECTED OFFICIALS. IN 1970 THERE WERE ONLY 240.

IF THINGS WERE SO GOOD WHY DID DEADRIA FARMER-PAELLMANN START A ONE-WOMAN CAMPAIGN IN THE YEAR 2000, DEMANDING RESTITUTION AND APOLOGIES FROM MODERN COMPANIES THAT PLAYED A DIRECT ROLE IN ENSLAVING BLACK FOLKS?

THEY STILL DIDN'T COME UP OFF OF ANY MONEY.

SEE I TOLD YOU WE HAD A CASE FOR REPARATIONS. AETNA JUST APOLOGIZED FOR ITS ROLE IN THE SLAVE TRADE. IT'S THE FIRST OF ITS KIND.

YOU HAVE TO START SOMEWHERE.

AND DON'T TELL ME ABOUT ELECTED OFFICIALS.

BUT IT'S ONLY TWO O'CLOCK IN THE AFTERNOON.

SORRY UNCLE, THE POLLS ARE CLOSED.

... DIDN'T DO US ANY GOOD IN FLORIDA DURING THE 2000 PRESIDENTIAL ELECTIONS.

NOBODY SAID IT WAS EASY, BUT PROGRESS IS PROGRESS, AND THE NEW MILLENIUM BROUGHT ABOUT HISTORIC DEVELOPMENTS FOR BLACK PEOPLE IN LEADERSHIP POSITIONS IN MAINSTREAM AMERICA: COLIN POWELL AND CONDOLEEZA RICE BECAME THE FIRST 2 BLACK SECRETARY OF STATES, KEN CHENAULT WAS NAMED CEO OF AMERICAN EXPRESS AND DICK PARSONS WAS NAMED CEO OF TIME WARNER.
WHILE VISIONARY URBAN ENTREPENEURS LIKE FORMER BASKETBALL GREAT EARVIN "MAGIC" JOHNSON ARE AT THE FOREFRONT OF REVITALIZING MANY OF OUR COMMUNITIES.

THROW THAT IN WITH THE HUNDREDS OF BLACK MEN AND WOMEN THAT SIT ON CORPORATE BOARDS THROUGHOUT AMERICA,

AND IT'S PLAIN TO SEE THAT OUR INFLUENCE CONTINUED TO GROW.

CORPORATE AMERICA

INFLUENCE! IF WE HAVE SO MUCH INFLUENCE, THEN HOW COME THE US WASN'T REPRESENTED AT THE CONFERENCE ON RACISM THAT WAS HELD IN SOUTH AFRICA IN 2001? JUST 2 WEEKS AFTER THE 9/11 ATTACKS HAPPENED.

I KNOW YOU'RE NOT BLAMING THE 9/11 ATTACKS ON A LACK OF BLACK POLITICAL INFLUENCE

NO.

EVEN WITH THE HORRORS OF 9/11, BLACK PEOPLE STILL CONTINUED TO MAKE MOVES. RUTH SIMMONS ASSUMED THE PRESIDENCY OF BROWN UNIVERSITY AND IN JAN. 2002 STANLEY O'NEAL WAS NAMED THE CEO OF MERRILL LYNCH. SO I REPEAT, OUR INFLUENCE JUST KEPT ON GROWING. IN FACT ONE WRITER COINED THE PHRASE "BLACK POWER, INC" TO DESCRIBE OUR SUCCESSES IN THE UPPER ECHELONS OF FORTUNE 500 COMPANIES AND ELITE UNIVERSITIES.

YOU CAN CALL IT BLACK POWER, INC. I'M WATCHING BLACK POWER SHRINK... OH AND BY THE WAY, YOUR BOY STANLEY O'NEAL GOT THE BOOT FROM MERRILL LYNCH... AND IF DICK PARSONS ISN'T OUT OF TIME WARNER NOW, HE WILL BE SOON. KEEP TALKING.

WHATEVER, GETTING BACK TO 2002--IT WAS ALSO A BIG YEAR FOR BLACK FOLKS IN ENTERTAINMENT, AS DENZEL WASHINGTON AND HALLE BERRY WON THE BEST ACTOR AND BEST ACTRESS AWARD IN THE SAME YEAR.

ONE WINS FOR PLAYING A CROOKED COP, THE OTHER WINS FOR PLAYING A "NEAR TRAGIC & MULATTO THAT SLEEPS WITH A FUNNY-LOOKING WHITE MAN, AND YOU'RE CALLING IT HISTORY... NEXT THING YOU KNOW THEY'LL BE REMAKING BIRTH OF A NATION. YOU THINK 2002 WAS A BIG YEAR BECAUSE OF AWARDS, BUT I LIKED 2003 BETTER.

IS THAT RIGHT?

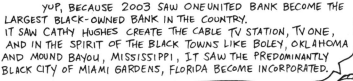

YUP, BECAUSE 2003 SAW ONE UNITED BANK BECOME THE LARGEST BLACK-OWNED BANK IN THE COUNTRY. IT SAW CATHY HUGHES CREATE THE CABLE TV STATION, TV ONE, AND IN THE SPIRIT OF THE BLACK TOWNS LIKE BOLEY, OKLAHOMA AND MOUND BAYOU, MISSISSIPPI, IT SAW THE PREDOMINANTLY BLACK CITY OF MIAMI GARDENS, FLORIDA BECOME INCORPORATED.

UNLIKE MANY PREDOMINANTLY BLACK CITIES IN THE COUNTRY, THAT CITY IS HOME TO MANY OF THE MAJOR ECONOMICS DRIVERS IN ITS HOME STATE, AND BEARS WATCHING... BUT YOU KNOW WHAT. LET ME MAKE MY POINT.

I WON'T DIMINISH THE FACT THAT OUR PEOPLE HAVE DONE AMAZING THINGS IN THIS COUNTRY AGAINST SIGNIFICANT RESISTANCE, BUT THESE ARE STILL LARGELY INDIVIDUAL ACCOMPLISHMENTS.

*

SMAK!

211

AND TO MAKE MATTERS WORSE, EVEN WITH THE EMERGENCE OF SUPERSTAR POLITICIANS LIKE LEGITIMATE PRESIDENTIAL CANDIDATE BARACK OBAMA, THE NATIONAL PROFILE OF OUR STRUGGLE CONTINUES TO BE MORE ABOUT FIGHTING COURT CASES THAN ANYTHING ELSE AND A FEW OF OUR LEADERS LOOK MORE LIKE AMBULANCE CHASERS THAN STATESMEN.

IT'S TIME FOR A CHANGE IN STRATEGY AND YOU ALL DON'T REALIZE IT.

TO SHOW HOW INGRAINED THIS MINDSET HAS BECOME, BRUCE GORDON, LEFT THE NAACP EARLY IN 2007 BECAUSE HE WAS UNABLE TO GET THE NAACP TO EXPAND ITS PHILOSOPHY BEYOND THE NARROW FOCUS OF LITIGATION THAT WAS INITIATED BY WALTER WHITE IN 1933.

THE BIOGRAPHY OF W.E.B DUBOIS

DAVID LEVERING LEWIS

FUNNY HOW HISTORY REPEATS ITSELF, W.E.B DUBOIS HAD THE SAME ISSUE 74 YEARS AGO.
STILL THIS IS NO TIME FOR A PITY PARTY. OUR HISTORY IS OUR COLLECTIVE SPIRIT, MEMORY AND IMAGINATION. WE CAN LOOK BACK AT IT FOR WISDOM, BUT ALSO TO LEARN FROM OUR MISTAKES AND MISSED OPPURTUNITIES, FOR INSTANCE, EVEN THE NAACP HAS HAD MOMENTS IN THE LAST 74 YEARS, WHERE IT'S THOUGHT OUT OF THE BOX. HOW MANY FOLKS HAVE HEARD OF MOUND BAYOU, MISSISSIPPI PHYSICIAN AND ENTREPENEUR DR. TRM HOWARD?

213

MR. WILKINS, YOU KNOW HOW BAD IT IS DOWN HERE IN MISSISSIPPI, BUT THE PEOPLE DO HAVE RESOURCES. I'M SURE IF THE NAACP SANCTIONED MY PROPOSAL OF PULLING OUR MONEY OUT OF THE WHITE BANKS, AND PUTTING THEM IN THE NEGRO OWNED TRI STATE NATIONAL, FOLKS WOULD DO IT.

MR. HOWARD, THIS ISN'T TYPICALLY THE TYPE OF THING, THE NAACP DOES. BUT YOU HAVE MY WORD, WE'LL SUPPORT THIS!

BECAUSE OF DR. TRM HOWARD'S PROPOSAL AND THE NAACP'S ACCEPTANCE OF IT, BLACK FOLKS IN MISSISSIPPI WERE ABLE TO WITHSTAND A RACIST CREDIT SQUEEZE INITIATED BY THE WHITE CITIZEN'S COUNCIL. OF COURSE A SHORT TIME LATER, DUE TO THREATS ON HIS LIFE, DR. HOWARD HAD TO RELOCATE TO CHICAGO.

AND HERE'S ANOTHER HISTORICAL GEM. HOW ABOUT WHAT TWO OF THE RICHEST BLACK MEN IN AMERICA, SAM FULLER AND AG GASTON PROPOSED TO MARTIN LUTHER KING JR. DURING THE PEAK OF THE MONTGOMERY BUS BOYCOTT?

DR. KING, YOUR BOYCOTT IS WORKING SPLENDIDLY. THE BUS COMPANY IS LOSING ALL KINDS OF MONEY AND IS READY TO SELL. AG AND I ARE READY TO PUT AN OFFER ON THE TABLE TO BUY THE COMPANY.

THAT'S RIGHT DR. KING. IMAGINE A NEGRO OWNED BUS COMPANY RIGHT HERE IN MONTGOMERY! THOSE WHITE FOLKS WOULD NEVER MESS WITH US AGAIN! WE COULD EVEN PUT THE WHITE FOLKS IN THE BACK IF WE WANTED.

GENTLEMEN, I APPRECIATE YOUR IDEA, BUT I'M NOT SURE IT'S GOING TO WORK, THE WHITE BACKLASH MIGHT BE TOO MUCH FOR US TO HANDLE.

MARTIN LUTHER KING JR. NEVER GOT BEHIND THE IDEA, AND OBVIOUSLY THE MONTGOMERY BUSES NEVER BECAME BLACK OWNED, BUT YOU HAVE TO LOVE THE IDEA. THE PLAIN TRUTH IS, THERE'S NOTHING STOPPING ANY OF US FROM USING LESSONS FROM HISTORY AND CREATIVELY APPLYING THEM TODAY.

216

Acknowledgements

*T*his book would not have been possible without Heidi von Schreiner, who had the vision of telling African-American history in comic book format. Thank you Alane Salierno Mason, our editor at Norton, for always demanding the best from us. For reading through thousands of pages of manuscript—to ensure that Roland's writing was accurate yet engaging—thank you Stephen Francoeur of The Philip Lief Group, Earl Lewis of the University of Michigan, Charles Johnson, and Nell Painter of Princeton University.

The phenomenal Maya Angelou inspired more than the title of our book. Her poem "Still I Rise" guided our entire narrative. Thank you Dr. Angelou for generously permitting us to use *Still I Rise* as the title for our work and lines from it as our epigraph.

For inspiration, thank you poets Nikki Giovanni and Sonia Sanchez; writers Lerone Bennett, Jr., Ralph Ellison, John Hope Franklin, Nelson George, Toni Morrison, and Ishmael Reed; and musicians James Brown, John Coltrane, and Rakim.

For their unwavering support, thanks to our parents Roland and Annis Laird, Ella Mae Dawson, and Celeste Gramby Bey. For not laughing at our comic book dreams, we love you Auntie Jeanne and Uncle Guy Cozier, and Jeanne and Michael Halyard. Special thanks to good friends Darryl Clark, David Stephen Hope, Rita Inskeep Storey, Leon Johnson, Nicole Nzuri King, Audrey "The AK" Kirnon, Bruce Lake, Jennifer Lee, Malik Maazi, Cosby B. Smiley, Gregory Smith, Darryl Stith, and Talib Yakini.

Thanks to all in the media who supported us when we were peddling Posro comic books and strips, especially the black press and radio. Thank you curator Rochon Perry for putting Posro in the company of legendary black cartoonists in the Black Ink exhibit at the Cartoon Art Museum in San Francisco.

We'd like to give a shout out to former intern Faraja Kennerly and past Posro artists Neil Errar, Jason Scott Jones, and Malcolm Williams. You guys are forever family—call home.

Extra special thanks to Christopher "Kortez" Robinson, Jimmy Eugene, and Raffy for assisting Adofo with the inkwork in *Still I Rise*.

Roland Laird
Taneshia Nash Laird
Elihu "Adofo" Bey

Bibliography

Aptheker, Herbert, ed. *A Documentary History of the Negro People in the United States.* 7 vols. New York: Citadel, 1994.

Asante, Molefi K., and Mark T. Mattson. *The Historical and Cultural Atlas of African Americans.* New York: Macmillan, 1991.

Axelrod, Alan, and Charles Phillips. *What Every American Should Know About American History: Two Hundred Events That Shaped the Nation.* Holbrook, MA: Bob Adams, 1992.

Bennett, Lerone, Jr. *Before the Mayflower: A History of Black America.* 6th ed. New York: Viking Penguin, 1993.

Burt, McKinley, Jr. *Black Inventors of America.* Portland, OR: National Book Company, 1969.

Christian, Charles M. *Black Saga: The African American Experience.* Boston: Houghton Mifflin, 1995.

Cowan, Tom, and Jack Maguire. *Timelines of African-American History: 500 Years of Black Achievement.* New York: Berkley, 1994.

Ferguson, Leland. *Uncommon Ground: Archaeology and Early African America, 1650–1800.* Washington, DC: Smithsonian Institution Press, 1992.

Franklin, John Hope, and Alfred A. Moss, Jr. *From Slavery to Freedom: A History of Negro Americans.* 7th ed. New York: Alfred A. Knopf, 1994.

Frazier, E. Franklin, and C. Eric Lincoln. *The Negro Church in America.* New York: Schocken Books, 1974.

Hamilton, Kenneth Marvin. *Black Towns and Profit: Promotion and Development in the Trans-Appalachian West, 1877–1915.* Urbana: University of Illinois Press, 1991.

Harding, Vincent. *There Is a River.* New York: Harcourt, Brace, Jovanovich, 1992.

Hine, Darlene Clark, Elsa Berkley Brown, and Rosalyn Terborg Penn. *Black Women in America: An Historical Encyclopedia.* 2 vols. Bloomington: Indiana University Press, 1994.

Hine, Darlene Clark, Linda Reed, and Wilma King. *We Specialize in the Wholly Impossible: A Reader in Black Woman's History.* Brooklyn, NY: Carlson Publishing, 1995.

James, Portia. *The Real McCoy: African-American Invention and Innovation, 1619–1930*. Washington, DC: Smithsonian Institution Press, 1989.

Katz, William Loren. *Black Indians: A Hidden Heritage*. New York: Simon and Schuster, 1986.

———. *The Black West: A Documentary History of African-American Westward Expansion of the United States*. New York: Simon and Schuster, 1996.

Lincoln, C. Eric. *The Black Church Since Frazier*. New York: Schocken Books, 1974.

Litwack, Leon, and August Meier, eds. *Black Leaders of the Nineteenth Century*. Urbana: University of Illinois Press, 1988.

Marable, Manning. *Beyond Black and White: Rethinking Race in American Politics and Society*. London: Verso, 1995.

———. *How Capitalism Underdeveloped Black America*. Boston: South End Press, 1983.

Meier, August, and Elliott Rudwick. *From Plantation to Ghetto*. 3rd ed. New York: Hill and Wang, 1976.

Morgan, Edmond S. *American Slavery–American Freedom: The Ordeal of Colonial Virginia*. New York: W.W. Norton, 1975.

Moses, Wilson J. *The Golden Age of Black Nationalism, 1850–1925*. New York: Oxford University Press, 1988.

Nash, Gary. *The Private Side of American History: Readings in Everyday Life*. New York: Harcourt, Brace, Jovanovich, 1975.

Nash, Gary, Julie Roy Jeffrey, John R. Howe, Peter J. Frederick, Allen F. Davis, and Allan M. Winkler. *The American People: Creating a Nation and a Society*. 3rd ed. 2 vols. New York: HarperCollins College Publishers, 1994.

Painter, Nell. *Sojourner Truth: A Life, a Symbol*. New York: W. W. Norton, 1996.

Quarles, Benjamin. *The Negro in the Making of America*. New York: Macmillan, 1987.

Rivlin, Gary. *Fire on the Prairie: Chicago's Harold Washington and the Politics of Race*. New York: Henry Holt, 1992.

Tindall, George B., and David E. Shi. *America: A Narrative History*. 3rd ed. 2 vols. New York: W. W. Norton, 1993.